MOM
IN THE
MOVIES

THE ICONIC SCREEN MOTHERS YOU LOVE

(AND A FEW YOU LOVE TO HATE)

TURNER CLASSIC MOVIES

BY RICHARD CORLISS

Foreword by Debbie Reynolds and Carrie Fisher

SIMON & SCHUSTER

NEW YORK LONDON TORONTO SYDNEY NEW DELHI

This book is for Mary Corliss, its inspirer and first reader, who helped choose the films and photographs and poured her loving critical acuity into the entire process; and for Priscilla Painton, Shannon Clute and Sydney Tanigawa—the three glorious godparents of *Mom in the Movies*.

—Richard Corliss

Simon & Schuster
1230 Avenue of the Americas
New York, NY 10020

First Simon & Schuster hardcover edition April 2014

SIMON & SCHUSTER and colophon are registered trademarks of Simon & Schuster, Inc.

For information about special discounts for bulk purchases, please contact
Simon & Schuster Special Sales at 1-866-506-1949 or business@simonandschuster.com.

The Simon & Schuster Speakers Bureau can bring authors to your live event.
For more information or to book an event, contact the Simon & Schuster Speakers Bureau at
1-866-248-3049 or visit our website at www.simonspeakers.com.

Interior design by Ruth Lee-Mui
Jacket design by Marc Cohen
Jacket photographs: Front (left to right), *Changeling, Erin Brockovich, The King and I* courtesy of Photofest;
A Raisin in the Sun courtesy of Everett Collection. Back (left to right), *Aliens* courtesy of Photofest; *Mildred Pierce* courtesy of Turner Theatrical Library; *Forrest Gump, Lorenzo's Oil* courtesy of Everett Collection.

Manufactured in the United States of America

1   3   5   7   9   10   8   6   4   2

Library of Congress Cataloging-in-Publication Data

Corliss, Richard.
Mom in the movies : the iconic screen mothers you love (and a few you love to hate) /
by Richard Corliss ; foreword by Debbie Reynolds and Carrie Fisher ; [with editorial assistance
from Turner Classic Movies].—First Simon & Schuster hardcover edition.
pages   cm
1. Mothers in motion pictures.   I. Turner Classic Movies (Firm)   II. Title.
PN1995.9.M63C68   2014
791.43'65252—dc23   2013044850
ISBN 978-1-4767-3826-0
ISBN 978-1-4767-3828-4 (ebook)

Contents

Contents

MOM
IN THE
MOVIES

Foreword by
Debbie Reynolds and Carrie Fisher

Movie mothers are a topic near and dear to me for many reasons. I've been a movie admirer since I was a little girl and I have always loved my mother. I had the immense honor of working with marvelous actresses who played my mother from age seventeen, until I portrayed a mother myself in the movie *Mother*. And of course, I am a mother of two wonderful children, one of whom is likewise an actress and a mother.

I raised my children on the great old movies that always had delightful actors—great character actors, and especially great mothers. These movie mothers made my children happy, as they have so many children. If you had a difficult childhood, movie mothers depicted understanding, aided you through those hard years and gave you hope. How many of us wanted our *real* mothers to be more like our *reel* mothers, the ones we grew up with in the movies? I will guess all of us!

Greer Garson in *Mrs. Miniver* and Maureen O'Hara in *How Green Was My Valley*, Jane Darwell in *The Grapes of Wrath* and Margaret Wycherly in *Sergeant York*—to name just a few. We loved them all because of their wisdom and understanding, which always saved the day (and, more importantly, the children).

I was lucky when it came to both kinds of mothers, the real and the reel. My own mother instilled in me the desire to accomplish every project that I started and follow it through to its completion. Both of my parents were in agreement on that point. Also, always to follow "The Golden Rule" and be kind to everyone—that was her major influence on shaping me as a person, which I, in turn, have imparted to my own children. Her ideas and teachings have followed me throughout my life. I am very grateful to both of my parents for their love and guidance, which have served me well in both my career and life. But it's also fun for anyone to imagine being hugged and completely understood by a movie mother, who happens to be a marvelous actress and so loved by millions—and I had plenty of those experiences as well.

When I moved to MGM Studios, I got to work with Bette Davis as my mother in *The Catered Affair*. She was fabulous—powerful, yet helpful. Scary too, because she was always helping to teach you how to properly act, and she made every point a *strong* one. How I grew to adore her. She was a wonderful "second mother." MGM had all the beautiful actresses under contract, including the supporting actresses who never played the glamorous mothers, but the more supportive, loving, funny mothers.

My next movie mother was a lady by the name of Una Merkel. She was the sweetest and most loving of all. We remained great friends for many years afterward. Later, Lilli Palmer played my mother in the movie *The Pleasure of His Company*, with Fred Astaire and Tab Hunter. See? Just like that I had three new mothers!

Of course, I enjoyed watching movie mothers as much as I did working with them. My favorite was Spring Byington—so cute and cuddly, always understanding when others were critical. In *Presenting Lily Mars* she, or rather, her role, let you believe you could realize your dreams. And remember Irene Dunne in *I Remember Mama*? Among my other favorites were Myrna Loy, Agnes Moorehead, Dorothy McGuire, Sophia Loren, Jane Wyatt, Donna Reed and Norma Shearer.

The movie studios, of course, made a point of distinguishing between reel mothers and real mothers. The Breen Office and the Production Code forced married couples into separate beds on the set (how did they think these women became mothers?), and films could rarely depict motherhood in any way that was nearly so messy as it is in real life. Movie mothers were neat, organized, energetic, and seemed always ready to be a perfect spouse and parent. They made most of us forget the areas in our life we weren't so happy with, for a movie moment.

—Debbie Reynolds

The first awareness I had of what a family was came from the television show *Father Knows Best*. Robert Young played the role of the father, Mr. Anderson—the man who presumably knew best. Jane Wyatt portrayed the iconic 1960s television mother, always in the kitchen wearing her apron and making dinner, beaming proudly over her beloved brood. Somehow my memories of these characters are far more vivid than a lot of my recollections of my own relatives. The TV father would come home each evening dressed in a suit and tie, and pull his daughter onto his lap, giving her a hug and a kiss. He lovingly referred to his daughter as "Princess," a title that would become synonymous with me, but more on that another time. Their Princess, their kitten, their baby girl would grow up to be just like her mother but do more charity work and play tennis. She would never be too big to be Mommy and Daddy's favorite little girl.

I dreamt of having a family like this. Never mind that I had a beautiful mother all my own at home, who beamed proudly at my brother and me. My mother was nothing like Margaret Anderson, the mother character on *Father Knows Best*. She didn't wear an apron or serve homemade meals—well, until recently, but there is no apron involved when she makes dinner for her adored dog, Dwight. Not only that, I didn't have a father who knew best; he refused to hoist me onto the safe harbor of his lap and make it all better than okay. I found out later that *many* of my schoolmates lacked their own *Father Knows Best* families—we all lived in this media-made world where everyone grinned and lived happily ever after every day. Is it any wonder we all grew up to be serial killers or failed anorexics (if we were lucky) before the age of thirty-five?

It must have conveniently slipped my rebellious adolescent mind that I had my very own media mother at home. I really didn't *need* Margaret Anderson. I mean, let's face it, Margaret wasn't *prettier* than my mom, and both were loving and kind. What Margaret was that Debbie wasn't was *edited*. In addition, Margaret could cook, whereas my mother *had* a cook. My mother could *spell* apron; Mrs. Anderson just wore one. But kindness and aprons aside, I think the biggest difference is the editing. Editing rescues us from the tedium and upset of everyday life. I don't mean to suggest that my mother is boring and upsetting—beyond quite the opposite—but let's face it, *everyone* shares that *potential*. I know I do. Ask around.

Parents are rarely strangers, although my father was frequently the exception to that rule. It was *Father Knows Best* that taught me that my relationship with my male parent was many miles from ideal. So, media can teach us *something*, the welcome lesson of what we have versus the punishing ideal that whispers what we lack—what we endure, as opposed to what we desire. The odd thing was, because my mother, for the most part, could be found wandering through "Ideal Land," I was envied, as most kids my age only knew the edited, filmed version of Debbie Reynolds. I envied others, as I assumed they lived with the beaming, apron-clad Mrs. Anderson.

As far as I know, I've only played mothers a few times in my nuanced career as an actress. I truly wasn't certain of this fact until I looked myself up on IMDb, something I have to do these days in order to reminisce. The difficulty is that I try not to get too far into character when acting, as there's a chance I might be unable to easily extract myself later. Unfortunately, I can only say with absolute certainty that I was anyone's parent when I played Carol Peterson. My husband and I had a nine-year-old son named Dave. (I thought I had had *two* children, though according to IMDb, I had one. So you see, as the saying goes, you never know for *certain* how many children you have until you verify it online.) So, judging from my casting record, I wasn't *really* the maternal type. Which might explain why I only had one child in Actual Unedited Life. A fine example of life imitating art (or thereabouts), depending on whether or not you consider the movie *The 'Burbs* art, in which I played a Mrs. Anderson–type mother as Tom Hanks's wife.

According to my source at IMDb, I was in something called *From Here to Maternity*. Inspired by one of Anton Chekhov's early short stories (I'm lying), I'm *assuming* the piece related to women waiting to welcome their little stranger; so, though I wasn't a bona fide parent à la *The 'Burbs*, my guess is that I played a mother-to-be (that, or a gynecologist). Though I discovered it on IMDb as a credit of mine, the main things I found out were that it was a short and Richard Simmons was also in it, hopefully playing a pregnant person himself.

It turns out, not only have I not played a host of screen moms, I haven't *had* a lot of screen mothers. But then, how many do you really need? Lee Grant was my mother in *Shampoo*, though we didn't have any scenes together. Anne Bancroft played my mother-in-law in *Garbo Talks*, and last but far, far away from least, Natalie Portman portrayed the mother-to-be of my *Star Wars* character Princess Leia (alluded to earlier) *three times*.

But, though this was a fine assortment of moms, I must've felt cheated in some way, because once I began writing, the very first screenplay I wrote, *Postcards from the Edge*, included the mother of all mothers. I'm not bragging or anything. I'm just stating a fact. If you saw it, you'd know what I mean. It was the story of a mother and daughter. A mother and daughter in show business. As I recall, a certain amount of the dialogue in *Postcards* was actually taken from my relationship with my mother, from our Actual Unedited Life. Go figure.

All my life I'd watched mothers and daughters in films and either wished that my mother and I were at least a little more like them, as their characters trended toward the ideal, or was *thrilled* that we were as unlike them as we were.

Obviously, the relationships that appealed to me most could be found in black and white films (both speaking and silent), but they were also in Technicolor films and occasionally even modern-day color films—of the sentimental and/or old-fashioned variety.

Of course, the film relationships that made me feel even more grateful in the extreme for having Debbie Reynolds as a parent were in films such as *Mommie Dearest*, *Carrie*, and, of course, the classic mother-daughter tribute, *Nice Girls Don't Explode*, to name but a few.

Either way—whether you want to feel beat up and/or inspired by the seemingly ideal, filmed relationship, or thrilled and relieved by those cinematic torture-filled, murderous relationships—it's always interesting to shake out the cobwebs of your Actual Familial Female Intertwining (AFFI). It's never boring to check out someone else's idea of family life and see where you fall on the chaotic scale of art imitating life. See if by treating yourself to a mother-daughter film you can maybe even tip that scale, change your place on it or revel in the wonder of where you fell. Take leave of your Actual Unedited Life for a few hours and be anointed in entertainments of every style and type. You can never go wrong, even if you have to go wrong in a self-righteous way. My plan is to do a documentary of my mother and my life. That way we can document our actual life and pop in the editing later on—a kind of combination of real life and life of the artistic variety. Call it *Wash Out That Grey Gardens!* or *The Over Fifty Shades of Grey Gardens.*

—Carrie Fisher

INTRODUCTION

Where Have All the Mothers Gone?

I remember Mama. We called her Mom or Mother. Elizabeth McCluskey Corliss lived her entire long life in Philadelphia. For forty-one years Elizabeth taught first grade in the city's public school system; for thirty years she was married to the love of her life, my father, Paul, until his death in 1963; and for many more years she raised—uplifted—my brother, Paul Jr., and me, teaching us less by command than by example, by her easy charm and uncommon sense. I hardly exaggerate when I say that everyone who knew Elizabeth adored her, and that she repaid that affection a thousandfold. She loved her siblings, her sons, her grandchildren, her whole extended family and the friends she had accumulated over a gracious lifetime.

Her life, which lasted one hundred years, two months and twenty-two days—exactly the span of Gloria Stuart, the actress who played the older Rose in James Cameron's *Titanic*—wasn't all good luck: Within a year and a half in her mid-fifties she lost her husband and a breast to cancer. Her dear sister Margaret, who lived with us, died of cancer a few years later. But nothing dimmed Elizabeth's dimpled optimism, her belief in the decency of the people she knew. I knew most of them, and I agree they were good. Just not as wonderful as my mom.

Growing up in the 1950s, I imagined that my mother was the inspiration for television moms played by Donna Reed and Harriet Nelson, and that cheerful family programs like *Father Knows Best* were documentaries filmed with hidden cameras in our neighborhood. TV shows of that decade did what my parents did: teach, comfort and reassure. But who would make a movie of Elizabeth Corliss's life? In fifties films, I saw few women who reminded me of my mom. James Dean, who I thought nearly matched me in faunlike sensitivity, had a clueless mother in *Rebel Without a Cause* and a brothel-owning mother in *East of Eden*. A slew of serious films sprang from novels and plays that ripped the Band-Aid off generational wounds. No movie family convened as we did each evening in the living room, eating tuna salad on table trays and watching the evening news on a twelve-inch Philco set. The Corliss home life was surely worth living, I'll testify to that, but Hollywood might say it was not worth filming.

I sing the movie mother, proud and strong. Also warm and gentle and, on occasion, misguided or downright nasty. Motherhood has embraced multitudes across the history of the medium, from the earliest peep shows—when that regal mom Mary Queen of Scots was shown being beheaded in an 1895 trick film—through the 1930s–'40s golden age of both Hollywood and mothers, and up to the most modern films, when . . . Wait a minute, what happened? Where have all the mothers gone?

They should still be around, because they always have been. Mothers have driven dramatic literature from Euripides's *Medea* in 431 B.C. to Tyler Perry's Madea today. Ever since the Greeks, the theater has honored the compact between what any audience has experienced—the joys and tensions of the maternal bond—and what it can see onstage. Shakespeare knew that the actions of mothers could stoke classic tragedy: If Gertrude hadn't married her late husband's brother, her son, Hamlet, would have been just another morbid teen instead of a palace insurrectionist. In some of the great plays of the mid-twentieth century—*Death of a Salesman*, *Long Day's Journey into Night*, *A Raisin in the Sun* and *Who's Afraid of Virginia Woolf?*—women address their own or their husbands' infirmities and the urges of their children, real or imagined. In the last decade, Perry's touring plays about the sassy Mabel "Madea" Simpson, a character he says is based on his own mother and aunt, may not win drama awards, but they have extended into the twenty-first century the theater's fascination with mother love.

American television, for its entire lifespan, has teemed with mothers, from Lucy Ricardo and June Cleaver to Marge Simpson and *Breaking Bad*'s Skyler White. All have served as anchors of love, loyalty and common sense. Mostly, they serve at home, where the hearth is, and the TV set. The media room is near the kitchen, traditionally portrayed as Mom's domain, and the typical small-screen drama—a weekly habit, not an event—affirms her time-honored values: nurturing, reassurance, continuity, commitment. Learning and hugging, as the old TV rule goes. Mother knows best.

In films of the last half century, though, mothers have nearly become an endangered species. We grant that a modern superhero may have a mom: Thor (Chris Hemsworth) reveres his Fridda (René Russo); and in *Man of Steel*, Superman (Henry Cavill) has a birth mother (Ayelet Zurer) and an Earth mother (Diane Lane), both of them selflessly devoted to their boy. A villain, like the drug-cartel prince played by Ryan Gosling in *Only God Forgives*, may also have a mother: the cartel queen Kristin Scott Thomas, with a vicious mouth and a malicious will. But mainstream Hollywood has essentially consigned mother stories to foreign films (the Korean *Mother* and *Pieta*, for example) and to indie movies of the Sundance stripe (*Precious*, *The Kids*

Are All Right), which have inherited the domestic-drama genre that long sustained American cinema. In real life, mothers far outnumber superheroes or serial killers in this country—but not on this country's multiplex screens.

Why is the mother movie near extinction? Let us suggest a few reasons.

1. **Movies are about movement.** People *watch* TV but *go to* a movie. The big screen doesn't duplicate the cozy home viewing of TV; it's a giant wall for communal dreams. Having got out of the house, filmgoers presumably wanted to see the characters on that wall do the same: break out of the status quo to court danger and achieve physical triumph. The convention of womanly acceptance gave way to the depiction of manly quests. Unlike the theater and TV, media that from their beginnings embraced the power of the voice, cinema began in silence; it was all show, no talk. On a movie set, a crew member shouts, "Lights, camera, *action!*"—not "Lights, camera, *chatting.*"

   When sound films replaced silents in the late 1920s, they did become more like theater: filmed plays, in which people talked out their conflicts, often brilliantly. These were sophisticated wars of words, in an arena where women could battle men on equal terms, and win. But most of today's big movies are all show, little tell; they offer world-threatening scenarios resolved by rockets, space suits, muscles—in a word, manpower. Hollywood replaced weighty subjects with heavy lifting. Superheroes may *have* mothers, but they *aren't* mothers.

2. **The role of women has evolved.** For millennia, mothers have superbly performed crucial tasks—keeping the brood together, cooking and cleaning, instilling the values of civility and civilization—that were not seen as intrinsically cinematic; they were routine duties, drudge work, homework. In the last half century, the number of women in the workforce has risen sharply until it is now close to the percentage of employed men. That change should have cued a new era of movies about working women, including working mothers. But the demographic trend coincided with the ebbing of movie realism and the blooming of fantasy; we're talking about you, *Star Wars*. The

mammoth success of that sci-fi epic, surely the single most influential movie of the past forty years, certified Hollywood's flight away from women (and mothers) and toward heroic sons (with father issues).

The increased economic power of women meant only that they had more money to spend on movies about science-fiction and pulp-fiction men. If women wanted to see the drama and fun of a working mother's life in fictional form, they watched TV. In the rare cases when a woman is at the center of some big action picture, she is usually the solitary warrior, as unencumbered by children as any Marvel man. Katniss Everdeen couldn't win the Hunger Games if she had to go home at sundown to cook the kids' dinner.

3. **The audience has evolved.** For generations, when moviegoing was a family activity, Hollywood designed its films to appeal to all and offend few. In the half century of feature filmmaking before the industry introduced its rating system in 1968, anyone of any age could see any movie; that fact imposed a self-censorship on filmmakers and a modicum of good behavior on film content. Even in the early years of G-, PG-, R- and X-rated movies, Hollywood believed that, when a dating couple was considering what to see at the Bijou, the woman usually made the choice. Today, that rule doesn't apply so much. Movies are still a relatively cheap date, but women tend to go in groups to see a women's movie (*Sex and the City*, *Mamma Mia!*) and men go in packs to see guy movies (everything else). Since men, young men, are the crucial demographic in a hit franchise, Hollywood produces stories to appeal to their fantasy self-image.

And that's just in North America. In the rest of the world—a huge market that accounts for more than half of the business for pictures produced by the big studios—audiences don't care about the niceties of dialogue, especially as spoken by women with children. The global box office seems to validate this gender prejudice. Of the seventeen films that had earned more than a billion dollars at the worldwide box office through the end of 2013, the top two—James Cameron's *Avatar* and *Titanic*—were, yes, love stories of the Romeo-and-Juliet stripe, on the Atlantic or in outer space, but the heroine's mother in *Titanic* was the merest marplot. And *Titanic*, unlike *Star Wars*, was seen as a fluke, not a blueprint for a new spate of fateful romances. In the other billion-dollar movies, mothers were usually poignantly distant memories (as with Harry Potter's late mum) or nonexistent. Only the James Bond film *Skyfall* boasted a significant maternal figure: Judi Dench's M, the stern surrogate mom to both 007 and the movie's villain, Silva. Otherwise, it's all superheroes, pirates, wizards and Mad Hatters.

That list is tabulated by dollars, which have inflated as ticket prices soared over the decades. But the true measure of a film's success is tickets sold, and by this standard, five of the all-time top ten films contain significant maternal figures. In tenth place, *Snow White and the Seven Dwarfs*: a wicked stepmother, scheming to kill a girl who learns to mother seven small bachelors. At nine, *The Exorcist*: a single mother battles her child's possession by demons. At eight, *Doctor Zhivago*: the search for the lost child of the good doctor and his vibrant love Lara. At three, *The Sound of Music*: the nun postulant who becomes the wonderful, *singing* stepmother of seven starchy Austrian kids. And at number one, in what is still the most popular of all films, *Gone With the Wind*, with three prime maternal roles: Scarlett, the willful belle whose motherhood is creased by tragedy; Melanie, the saintly one, whose baby Scarlett midwifes; and Mammy, the house slave and Earth Mother of them all.

Turner Classic Movies knows the importance of *GWTW*. It was the first film shown on the network, as well as on its predecessor, TNT, when that channel was the flagship of the Ted Turner's MGM-RKO-Warner Bros. library. Moms still live in old movies, especially on TCM—which, if it shows a series of Irene Dunne or Fay Bainter films, can seem like Turner Classic Mothers. To look at the movies of Hollywood's golden age and beyond is to chart both the progression of women's power and the devolution of motherhood as the defining aspect of womanhood. Recalling the movies' saintly or sinful women, we hope to bring them back to life in all their heroism and travail, their wit and their passion.

This book will trace the course of movie mothers from their birth in silent films, through their flourishing in the golden age and into the thinning of the herd in later decades. These pages are graced by good moms and bad, stepmothers and surrogate mothers, maternal figures in crime movies, horror films and sci-fi epics. We don't guarantee that all your favorite movie mothers are included, but we offer more than a hundred for your edification and fond remembrance. You will revisit old friends; you may meet new ones. Where have the movie mothers gone? Here.

A word of warning: Any mother's story spans her whole life, and we sometimes tell what happens at the end, without the black flag of a **SPOILER ALERT**. But the appeal of these stories is less in their resolutions than in the details that give mood and meaning to any film. Mothers may die, but they'll never die out—not on TCM and not in this book, where we remember Mamas: mine, yours and the movies'.

The Human Comedy, 1943: Widowed mother Fay Bainter with her children
Donna Reed and Mickey Rooney and family friend Marsha Hunt.

A GALLERY OF GOLDEN AGE MOMS

*These actresses played women who were
heart strong and hearth warm.*

Golden Age Hollywood, which reveled in good women passing their finest qualities on to their young charges, boasted an informal stock company of actresses suitable for all manner of dear ladies; in memory they blend into a composite portrait of classic movie moms. Finding Fay Bainter, Beulah Bondi or Anne Revere in a film, audiences of the 1930s and '40s were instantly assured that maternal warmth awaited. At a higher level of marquee glamour, Myrna Loy and Irene Dunne proved ideal movie mothers: poised and caring, with a salutary leavening of worldly humor.

FAY BAINTER

Onstage from childhood, she trod the boards for thirty-five years before getting her first movie role, at forty, as Lionel Barrymore's wife and the mother of two grown children in the 1934 film *This Side of Heaven*. Bainter executed a diversionary maneuver as Bondi's impatient daughter-in-law in 1937's *Make Way for Tomorrow* (see the chapter "Bad Seeds") before solidifying her primacy as Hollywood's most motherly mother, with large eyes that cooed with empathy and the fret lines that were a concerned mom's war scars. She nurtured William Holden in *Our Town* (1940); twice served as Mickey Rooney's mother, in *Young Tom Edison* (1940) and *The Human Comedy* (1943); and played an Iowa farm woman shepherding her children Jeanne Crain and Dick Haymes in Rodgers and Hammerstein's *State Fair* (1945). As if testing the tensile strength of Bainter's characters, the studios often multiplied her children and amped up her woes. Warners transferred the Lane sisters and Gale Page from Claude Rains's care in *Four Daughters* to Bainter's in *Daughters Courageous* (1939). And in *Mrs. Wiggs of the Cabbage Patch* (1942) she is a shantytown mother with more kids than Ma Kettle and as many domestic challenges as Ma Joad. And she still managed to play it as comedy.

The essential Bainter films are two from 1938. ***Mother Carey's Chickens*** casts her as a Rhode Island "hen" who sustains her "chicks"—primarily, daughters Anne Shirley and Ruby Keeler—after the death of her sea captain husband. She imparts a mother's lore about first love to Shirley and scares away prospective buyers of the family's overmortgaged home by claiming the place is haunted. Offered the chance to live with their rich aunt, the daughters naturally stick with Mom. Anyone would—anyone who had seen ***White Banners***, in which Bainter is Hannah, a woman of mystery who brightens the Indiana lives of Paul and Marcia Ward (Rains and Kay Johnson) and their children with her good cooking, spot-on housekeeping and

White Banners, 1938: Fay Bainter intercedes between Claude Rains and the "neighbor boy" Jackie Cooper.

inspired hints for the inventions that Paul hopes to patent. Being a more genial Mary Poppins is only incidental to Hannah's secret mission: monitoring the progress of the Wards' neighbor boy Peter (Jackie Cooper), the child she had out of wedlock and was forced to abandon.

The performance earned Bainter a Best Actress Oscar nomination in the same year she won for Best Supporting Actress in a more worldly role as Bette Davis's aunt in *Jezebel*. Davis took Best Actress, and posterity wouldn't take it from her. But Bainter's work in *White Banners* deserves some award, for bringing shivering heartache and beneficence to Hannah, the constant mother and secular saint.

BEULAH BONDI

If Fay Bainter's face was a velvet pillow that welcomed a child's cuddles and cries, Beulah Bondi's was sharp, beaky, with small eyes and a thin mouth. Yet her features could crinkle with a memory of passion as Victor Moore's wife on their fiftieth wedding anniversary in *Make Way for Tomorrow*, or with rabid joy at the sight of a dear son, like Fred MacMurray in **Remember the Night** (1940). In that Preston Sturges script, directed by Mitchell Leisen, MacMurray is a Manhattan DA who has brought a shoplifting sharpie (Barbara Stanwyck) to his Indiana home for Christmas.

Like Bainter, Bondi came to movies in her forties, a ready-made mom. (In her 1931 film debut, *Street Scene*, she reprised her role as a tenement gossip in Elmer Rice's Broadway hit.) Often playing women far older than she, Bondi certified her golden age Mom status by serving as James Stewart's mother in four films, including three released within twenty months. In **Of Human Hearts** (1938) she is a minister's pioneer wife, Mary, selling precious silver spoons so her son Jason (Gene Reynolds as a boy) can read *Harper's Monthly*, and, a decade later, selling the family horse to buy a uniform for the grown Jason (Stewart) to wear as a Civil War doctor; even Abraham Lincoln intercedes to return a young man to his mother. Bondi and

facing page: Remember the Night, 1940: Fred MacMurray with his best girls, mother Beulah Bondi and aunt Elizabeth Patterson.

It's a Wonderful Life, 1946: James Stewart with Beulah Bondi as Ma Bailey and Samuel S. Hinds as his father, Peter.

Stewart were granted a comic respite in *Vivacious Lady* (1938), with the mother a friendly negotiator in the war between Stewart's jazzy bride Ginger Rogers and his stuffy father (Charles Coburn). The following year Bondi shone in the small, pivotal role of Ma Smith, the source of Senator Jimmy's humane grit in *Mr. Smith Goes to Washington*.

Bondi's last work with Stewart was her finest: spanning a quarter century as Ma Bailey to his George in Frank Capra's **It's a Wonderful Life** (1946). For most of the film she is the perfect mom, kissing George and saying, "That's for nothing," informing him of the crush his future wife Mary (Donna Reed) has on him and, when the Bailey Building & Loan fails, praying for the restoration of her boy's emotional equilibrium. Toward the end, in George's glimpse of Bedford Falls as the noir-Dickensian Pottersville, Bondi metamorphoses into the crone figure, suspicious and bitter, telling the son she never had that he should be in a lunatic asylum. A sepulchral vision of a town missing one small, crucial soul, this section of *It's a Wonderful Life* also suggests that the first requisite of a wonderful mother is the child into whom she can pour her love.

ANNE REVERE

Before Beulah Bondi got the part of Ma Bailey, Frank Capra had considered casting Anne Revere. But the actress, a direct descendant of Revolutionary War hero Paul Revere, was never short of mother roles—until she lost a later revolutionary war, when Hollywood blacklisted her in 1951. Some called her "Anne Severe" for her strong features worth chiseling on Mount Rushmore and for a glance that could penetrate platinum. And she played her share of forbidding biddies: the widow in *Sunday Dinner for a Soldier*, and Alice Faye's older sister in *Fallen Angel* (both 1945). Robert Rossen's **Body and Soul** (1947) casts her as Anna Davis, the proud, defiant mother of John Garfield's Charley, who, after his father dies, turns to boxing to support his urban-poor family. Abraham Polonsky's script sizzles with elemental mother-son exchanges. "I want money, *money*, MONEY!" Charlie tells Anna. And

National Velvet, 1943: Anne Revere encourages her horse-loving daughter Elizabeth Taylor.

when she spits out, "Better you go buy a gun and shoot yourself," he snaps back, "You need *money* to buy a gun!"

She mothered a saint—Bernadette of Lourdes (Jennifer Jones) in 1943's *The Song of Bernadette*—and an angel: Elizabeth Taylor, then twelve, in **National Velvet** (1944). As Mrs. Brown, she teaches Velvet a species of Hollywood moral relativism ("What's the meaning of goodness if there isn't a little badness to overcome?") and the value of pursuing unlikely goals. "We're alike," she tells her daughter. "I, too, believe that everyone should have a chance at a breathtaking piece of folly once in his life. . . . You're twelve; you think a horse of yours can win the Grand National. Your dream has come early; but remember, Velvet, it will have to last you all the rest of your life."

Gentleman's Agreement, 1947: Anne Revere counsels her son, Gregory Peck, on the stain of ethnic bigotry.

And as the mother of Gregory Peck, crusading journalist, in ***Gentleman's Agreement*** (1947), she both encourages her son to expose anti-Semitism and gently chides him for his own moderate sexism. All three of the roles earned Revere Oscar nominations for Best Supporting Actress. She won for *National Velvet*.

As Montgomery Clift's mother in *A Place in the Sun* (1951), her last film role before being blacklisted, Revere cedes pride of place to Taylor, now a ravishing eighteen-year-old, as the posh girl who purrs to her new beau, "Tell Mama. Tell Mama more."

MYRNA LOY

One of Hollywood's minor mysteries is why producers thought that Montana's very Anglo Myrna Williams—screen name, Myrna Loy—was suitable for roles of exotic mischief early in her career. In 1932 she played a malevolent Eurasian with hypnotic powers in *Thirteen Women* and Boris Karloff's sadistic daughter ("The whip! The whip!") in *The Mask of Fu Manchu*. Lucky for Loy, MGM's Irving Thalberg saw the affable modernity in the actress's screen presence; he teamed her with William Powell and Clark Gable in 1934's *Manhattan Melodrama*. She proved the perfect complement to each of these strong men, making seven films in all with Gable, fourteen with Powell, including the six *Thin Man* movies that stand today as the definitively breezy fantasy of modern marriage (see the "Serial Moms" chapter). Rarely top-billed, Loy shone as the wise mate with a bubbling intelligence and a high emotional IQ. In the words of the Cole Porter song that Richard Schickel used for the title of his TCM Loy tribute film in 1991, she was "so nice to come home to."

As Milly Stephenson in William Wyler's ***The Best Years of Our Lives*** (1946), she is the wife whom Fredric March's Al comes home to—beautifully visualized in the embrace of a reluctant warrior and the woman who has shared his ordeal from a continent away. During World War II, Loy had virtually retired from the screen to work for the Red Cross and other relief agencies. So the film, written by Robert E. Sherwood from MacKinley Kantor's verse novel, was a homecoming for Loy as well. Now forty-one, and having segued into mother roles, Loy is not different, simply more mature; Milly must counsel her daughter Peggy (Teresa Wright), who loves another veteran, the unhappily married Fred Derry (Dana Andrews). When Peggy, believing herself in a unique romantic dilemma, tells her parents they never had any trouble, Milly turns to Al and snaps back: "'We never had any trouble!' How many times have I told you I hated you, and believed it in my heart? How many times have you said you were sick and tired of me—that we were all washed up? How many times have we had to fall in love all over again?" She is describing a married life that Peggy never knew, and that audiences of that time had rarely seen in the movies.

A year later, in **The Bachelor and the Bobby Soxer**, Loy played Shirley Temple's older sister—older by twenty-three years, in real life, so it may as well have been a mother role. In this comedy about a teenager with a crush on a playboy, Loy winds up with Cary Grant, who would be her husband in **Mr. Blandings Builds His Dream House** (1948). Like *The Egg and I*, which spawned the *Ma and Pa Kettle* series, *Blandings* is a warning against city folk's dreams of a country home. For a change, Loy's Muriel Blandings is the source of exasperation rather than wifely wisdom. She drives husband Jim and the renovators daft with minute instructions on the color scheme ("Not just yellow—a very gay yellow, something bright and sunshiny"). And she expresses her concern for her two teenage daughters by insisting, "I refuse to endanger the lives of my children in a house with less than four bathrooms!"

The more familiar Loy—the lovely, flinty American mom—returned in **The Red Pony** (1949), John Steinbeck's story of a Salinas County ranch couple (Loy and Shepperd Strudwick) and their young son (Peter Miles) who yearns for, and finally gets, his pony. Loy's genial unflappability was tested—and she aced the test—as Lillian Gilbreth in **Cheaper by the Dozen** (1950). Like *Meet Me in St. Louis*, this movie was based on a memoir of a happy family and was set in the same house that MGM built for the Judy Garland film. (In a TV version of *Meet Me in St. Louis*, in 1959, Loy took the Mary Astor role, with Walter Pidgeon as her husband and Jeanne Crain, Jane Powell and Patty Duke as their daughters.)

Cheaper by the Dozen—which shares only its title with the two Steve Martin

Mr. Blandings Builds His Dream House, 1948: Myrna Loy leads husband Cary Grant and daughters Connie Marshall and Sharyn Moffett to their new country estate.

comedies of 2003 and 2005—mines its humor from the efforts of Lillian's husband Frank (Clifton Webb) to apply his theories of time-and-motion efficiency to his large brood. Lillian was Frank's partner in these studies, and continued his work after his death (shown in the sequel *Belles on Their Toes*, 1952). Given Myrna's light touch in the film, she is also the smiling referee between her husband's conservative edicts of dress and behavior and her children's pleas for access to the twentieth century. Lillian manages to assuage both factions, the way Loy so often found a golden mean in her film roles. Her chiding felt like a caress; her voice suggested common sense after a nice bath. She was the wife as good pal, the mother as best friend, the home any moviegoer would be grateful to share.

IRENE DUNNE

She could play lover, friend or mother, in cutting comedy or ennobling weepie. Her drawling smile semaphored a you've-got-to-be-kidding undercut to her dashing leading men. Earning renown in 1920s musicals—including the Jerome Kern–Oscar Hammerstein II–Edna Ferber classic *Show Boat*—Dunne entered films in her early thirties and quickly hit the mother lode. She earned her first of five Best Actress Oscar nominations as Sabra Cravat in **Cimarron**, the 1931 Best Picture winner taken from another of Ferber's multigenerational novels.

Joining her journalist husband Yancey (Richard Dix) in the Oklahoma territory in 1889, Sabra outlasts his male pride ("You shouldn't interfere when men are having a little friendly shootin'"), edits his newspaper under his name, raises a daughter (Nancy Dover) and eventually wins public office. In effect, she drags or lifts Oklahoma and feminism into the twentieth century. Yancey shows his pride and gratitude with this florid testament: "Wife and mother, stainless woman, hide me, hide me in your love." That might have been the epigram for *The Secret of Madame Blanche* (1933), a *Madame X*–ish story of a good woman wronged and persevering to raise her son (Douglas Walton) to become less like his vanished father and more like her. Such was the march of civility in women's films of the 1930s, or any Hollywood decade that took mother love seriously.

Dunne starred in three Kern movie musicals: *Roberta* (1935), the 1936 *Show Boat* remake—in which she plays Magnolia, the showstopper and single mom—and *High, Wide and Handsome* (1937). She also put her lilting laugh to sparkling use in such comedies as *Theodora Goes Wild* (1936), *The Awful Truth* (1937) and *My Favorite Wife* (1940), all of which come close to defining screwball comedy at its most raucous and refined. Comedy is a genre more concerned with courtship than with motherhood. But occasionally a lighthearted tryst took an abrupt left turn toward catastrophe— with Charles Boyer in *Love Affair* or Cary Grant in the all-time weepie **Penny Serenade**.

Dunne's Julie and Grant's Roger yearn for kids, but on a New Year's Eve in Tokyo, disaster strikes; as critic Donald Ritchie caustically put it, "hundreds are destroyed in an earthquake so that Irene Dunne's miscarriage may be successfully accomplished." With Julie unable to bear children, the couple must adopt, and they find an infant that kindly Beulah Bondi says is "like no other in the world." Bondi means that the girl, Trina, is unique because she is theirs. As the clueless Julie and Roger cope with raising a child, and the story continues to pirouette between slapstick and tragedy, *Penny Serenade* confronts issues that can drive a loving couple apart. Cementing Julie's resolve are vintage pop songs that remind her of episodes in Peter's and her life and that underline Noël Coward's tart, truthful observation in *Private Lives*: "Extraordinary how potent cheap music is." Dunne's performance is equally potent, and not cheap but priceless.

In a movie career that lasted little more than twenty years, ending with the minor comedy *It Grows on Trees* in 1952, Dunne played good mothers with the same lithe determination she had brought to her portrayal of a feisty daughter-in-law in *The Silver Cord* (see the chapter "Malevolent Moms"). She was the American nurse in wartime London, hoping that her soldier son did not meet the fate of her World War I husband, in **The White Cliffs of Dover** (1944). She served as teacher and surrogate mom to the children of monarch Rex Harrison in *Anna and the King of Siam* (1946). She deflated William Powell's bluster in *Life with Father* (1947) and a year later incarnated the beatific Norwegian matriarch in *I Remember Mama* (see the

Penny Serenade, 1941: Beulah Bondi makes Irene Dunne and Cary Grant
the new parents of the infant Trina (Baby Biffle).

The White Cliffs of Dover, 1944: World War II nurse Irene Dunne tends to her soldier son, Peter Lawford.

chapter "The Great American Mom"). All three of these films were based on biographies of real women who held their families—and, in Anna Leonowens's case, an Asian country—together with the gifts of tact and stubbornness. But could any of them have radiated Irene Dunne's easy, enduring grace? And who could sing her babies a lovelier lullaby?

Motherhood in the Movies

Growing up, the films of my mother's that made an impression on me at that time were mainly from the Warner Bros. years—a time when the parts she was playing were about as far from motherhood as I could imagine. As a result, I simply couldn't identify the person whom I called "Mom" as the same person I saw on-screen. And because the sixties and seventies were such a time of change in the business of movies, yet still very much dominated by men on-screen, I was confronted by many more screen fathers than mothers.

It was the discovery of Beulah Bondi in *It's a Wonderful Life* (1946) that helped me to understand more fully these difficult constraints placed on movie mothers. While she was the very thread of motherhood that ran through the thirties and forties, what struck me about her character in *It's a Wonderful Life* was not her time on-screen as a mom—despite her success as an actor at injecting humanity into a stock "mom" character—but rather her appearance in George Bailey's nightmare Bedford Falls, had he not been born. Mary Bailey as a spinster was closed, pinched, afraid. Unhappy in capital letters, without the joy of motherhood, we were told. Reinforcing this theme was Violet, played by Gloria Grahame, who was decidedly not a mother either in the actual Bedford Falls or in George's nightmarish vision. Her character's only option was, short of full emancipation, to be a fallen woman. While there is no denying Frank Capra's unparalleled ability to open up the inner recesses of an audience's emotions, this was a decidedly male point of view on motherhood, and the lack thereof.

My godmother, Katie Hepburn, a paragon of an independent woman as Eleanor of Aquitaine in *The Lion in Winter* (1968), jumped out at me as a newer type of mother. Sure of herself, with an unquenchable ambition not only of her own but for her favorite son as well. Yet a prisoner of her ambition, her upbringing and, quite literally, her husband the king. Her own woman, but again, only to a point—ultimately defined by men.

It would be years before the art form would give us the two screen mothers who, for me, stood out the most: Dianne Wiest in *Parenthood* (1989) and Emma Thompson in *Love Actually* (2003) were actual, fully formed women. Wiest had recently played a character who was so emotionally needy, in *Hannah and Her Sisters* (1986), that it was jarring and thrilling to see her as a mother who was there for her kids. Not just there, but able and willing to talk to them on their terms and not afraid to not know the answers. Emma Thompson, whose performance gave *Love Actually* a real emotional foundation, was so completely present and fully committed to her marriage and children that I couldn't understand Alan Rickman's infidelity to her, despite his secretary's attributes. But I completely understood her willingness to remain in that marriage, doing the dirty work that men are sometimes unable to. That, it seems, is motherhood.

And yet, screen parents carry just as much power in their absence as well. After seeing Cecil Kellaway's character in *Harvey* (1950) talk about his wish to return to the Akron of his youth, I was fascinated about his character's upbringing there, so golden and safe that he would willingly return. What created that warm memory? How did he grow up? Clearly in the arms of a loving mother and father.

—Sam Robards

Madame Butterfly, 1915: America's Sweetheart, Mary Pickford, as a suffering young Japanese mother.

SILENT MOMS

*The cinema's first female stars brought
a girlish poignancy to maternal love.*

Imagine, at the dawn of the twentieth century, entering an arcade or music hall for the first glimpse of that new mechanical marvel: the motion picture. Or, in the 1920s, a visit to that true cathedral of commerce, the movie palace. In a lavish auditorium seating up to four thousand people, the lights would dim, and on a huge screen, magic would ensue. To a generation of Americans, home-bred or immigrant, silent movies provided the kind of iridescent spectacles that a mother gifted in storytelling might enthrall her child with at bedtime. Those theaters were the world-wide audience's womb, nursery, babysitter and mom.

The first American films, created in the 1890s by Thomas Edison's company to be shown as "peep shows" in arcades, were documentaries, lasting only a few seconds each, that showed the manly spectacles of blacksmiths hammering, athletes flexing their muscles, firemen at a blazing house, combatants in a boxing ring. Women appeared infrequently and sensationally in Edison's early pictures. The 1895 film ***The Execution of Mary, Queen of Scots*** employed trick photography to portray the beheading of the monarch (and mother of the future king of England); it may be the first mother movie *and* the first splatter film. In the notorious *Fatima, Muscle Dancer*, the skimpily dressed performer whirls and shimmies, and when the shaking of bosom and booty reaches its climax, two censorious rows of fence posts are painted on the image to obscure the action.

In 1896 Edison released its most popular picture of the decade, and one of its first to be viewed not through a peephole but on a large screen. A twenty-second excerpt from the Broadway play *The Widow Jones*, it featured two heavyset, middle-aged stage actors, May Irwin and John C. Rice, embracing, silently chatting and finally smooching. The movie, known as ***The Kiss***, stoked a furor because of its intimacy: the two figures in medium close-up (instead of the standard long shot) engaged in a traditionally private moment. Here was the forerunner of every love story, romantic comedy and by extension—if the kiss were to lead to kids—motherhood drama.

As the form attracted larger audiences by expanding into music halls, then storefront nickelodeons and finally theaters across the land—and as filmmakers like D. W. Griffith enlarged the cinematic vocabulary—movies might have acknowledged that half of their constituency was female, and that 100 percent had mothers. Yet the masters of this new medium, invented after most of its customers had been born, sensed that they should offer dreams of escape: leaving home to discover the manifest destiny of a happy ending.

The early film entrepreneurs also realized that the old would rather watch the young than the young the old. The harsh lighting of the first motion picture cameras punished the faces of middle-aged stage stars (like Rice and Irwin) while idealizing the features of girleens and college-age men. Beauty was youth, youth beauty; that twist on Keats's adage is all the movies knew on earth, and all they needed to know.

GRIFFITH'S GIRLS

The first movie-bred performer to become famous was Florence Lawrence. Born Florence Bridgwood in Hamilton, Ontario, she was barely eighteen when she joined Biograph Studios, where D. W. Griffith was the house director. (For mother roles—in nearly 200 shorts and features covering the entire span of his twenty-three-year film career—he cast the flinty, saintly Kate Bruce.) Lawrence appeared with John R. Cumpson, then more than twice her age, in eleven "Mr. and Mrs. Jones" shorts, directed by Griffith, about the comic misadventures of a young married couple. In one film, *The Peachbasket Hat*, a Jones baby shows up, but only as the prop in a farcical confusion involving the couple's maid and her gypsy friends.

At the time, film actors were not publicly identified (neither were the directors or crew). Carl Laemmle would change that. He signed Lawrence to his Independent Moving Pictures Company (IMP) and promoted her into celebrity with an outrageously effective publicity stunt: spreading the rumor that she had died, then announcing, "We nail the lie," and producing his new star in the flesh. Lawrence moved to two other studios but by 1916 had been supplanted by *real* actors, *real* stars: Lillian Gish and Mary Pickford, both discovered by Griffith while still in their teens. Lawrence sank into bit parts—one of her last was a townsperson in the Barbara Stanwyck film *So Big!* (1932)—and died a suicide in 1938 at age fifty-two.

Laemmle had made Lawrence a famous name, but Mary Pickford virtually invented movie stardom. Tutored on Broadway and at Biograph, where she made 132 short films directed by Griffith between 1909 and 1912, Pickford was the first to kindle the wildfire of the film public's ardor; Charlie Chaplin, who would achieve even greater renown, made his mark slightly later. Fans mobbed Pickford; they fetishized her luxuriant curls; they bought massage creams and calendars with her face on them. And though she was known for playing cute or pathetic little girls, it was the five-foot pixie who first made the moguls pay huge sums for talent. "No, I really cannot afford to work for only $10,000 a week," she coyly told Adolph Zukor of Famous Players in 1916, back when that was real money. Although she never took a director's credit, she supervised every aspect of her films. And in 1919, as the cofounder of United Artists with Griffith, Chaplin and her soon-to-be husband Douglas Fairbanks, Pickford showed the canniest business sense.

"America's Sweetheart," like her predecessor Florence Lawrence, was Canadian. Pickford was born in Toronto in 1892, as Gladys Smith, to a father who died when she was five and a stage mother, Charlotte, determined to raise her three children out of poverty. Mary and her siblings, Jack and Lottie, all became actors, and Charlotte remained Pickford's closest adviser. (Mary faced the moneymen without an agent or manager.) Hidden under the celebrated ringlets, Pickford's adding-machine brain calculated that the worldwide audience would pay to see moral tales of girls—Stella Maris, Amarilly of Clothes-Line Alley, Pollyanna, Little Annie Rooney—who grew up poor, as she had, colliding with the rich and ultimately instructing them that the lower class is not a lower species. Far from being lace valentines, many of her films exposed the crimes of orphanages run like penitentiaries and the tragedies of children allowed to die from inhumanity or neglect. Like Dickens, Pickford wed sentiment to social passion and created enduring popular art.

Frozen in a simulated preadolescence for most of her silent-film career, "Little Mary" specialized in sweet, spunky teens and tweens. (Four of the milder literary properties she filmed when she was in her twenties—*The Poor Little Rich Girl*, *Rebecca of Sunnybrook Farm*, *The Little Princess* and *Daddy-Long-Legs*—were remade as talkies for the child star Shirley Temple.) Occasionally Pickford would wander from her prototype to play a young mother. She was not quite convincing as the Japanese heroine in the 1915 **Madame Butterfly**, but the film did honor the ending of the original story by having Cho-Cho-San kill herself when she realizes her Western lover will not stay with her and their infant.

In **Little Lord Fauntleroy** (1921), Pickford essayed two roles: Cedric Errol, the poor American boy who becomes an English aristocrat, and his beloved widowed mother. (One shot, a miracle of double exposure, shows Pickford the boy leaning in to kiss Pickford the mother.) And in **Tess of the Storm Country**, which she made in 1914 and again in 1922, the Pickford character is a poor squatter who selflessly claims as her own the illegitimate baby of the landowner's daughter. Refused milk for the dying infant, Tess sneaks into a church to perform an emergency baptism—a surrogate mother's final brave gesture.

Pickford is again an impromptu mom in director William Beaudine's ***Sparrows*** (1926), perhaps the finest of her surviving films. On a baby farm, where cash-strapped parents have sent the children they can't afford to raise, Molly protects nearly a dozen younger unfortunates from the owner, an evil, limping hunchback named Grimes (Gustav von Seyffertitz). She is the only mother these waifs know—also their cheerleader, their teacher and scoutmistress and, when they must straddle a rickety tree branch across an alligator-infested swamp, their Indiana Jones. Too young for sexual fervor, Molly invests all her energy in mothering her forlorn charges. Yet Grimes will not give her enough food to keep them healthy: one infant dies of malnutrition, and Molly dreams that Jesus has come to take him to heaven. Fate finally intervenes in the guise of a wealthy widower whose baby Grimes had kidnapped and Molly has saved. When the baby cries out for Molly, the widower lets her and the whole orphan gang stay in his mansion. "You win, Mama Molly," he says. Another victory for Pickford, the mother of movie stardom.

If Pickford was the great female star of silent Hollywood, Lillian Gish was its greatest actress. Another child of a deserted mother who saw the theater as a way to support her family, Lillian moved in 1912 from Ohio to New York City, where Pickford introduced Lillian and her younger sister, Dorothy, to Griffith. Both Gish girls became popular performers, appearing together in Griffith's *Orphans of the Storm* (1921), but Dorothy was more the saucy soubrette, Lillian the elfin tragedian. Her wispy frame and doll face, dominated by soulful blue eyes, made Lillian ideal for demure young women who rise to heroism to battle life's disasters. She played the female lead in *The Birth of a Nation* (1915), though the men carried that Civil War story to its controversial climax in the founding of the Ku Klux Klan. In Griffith's ***Intolerance*** (1916), a film figure that interwove four stories across three millennia— think *Cloud Atlas*, but more wildly ambitious—Gish was the recurring figure of Eternal Motherhood, sitting next to a cradle, as Walt Whitman's lines from *Leaves*

Sparrows, 1926: Mary Pickford as the impromptu mom to the abandoned children in a Southern "baby farm."

of Grass ("Out of the cradle endlessly rocking . . . uniter of here and hereafter") crept across the screen.

Griffith's **Way Down East** (1920) was famous for its climax: Richard Barthelmess running across the ice floes on a frozen river to save Gish (who spent so much time collapsed on the sheet of ice that her right hand never fully regained its feeling). But Gish is the real elemental sensation as the poor, saintly Anna, seduced into a fake marriage by the rich roué Lennox Sanderson (Lowell Sherman), who abandons her when he learns she is pregnant. Scorned as a fallen woman at the moment her own loving mother has died, Anna is left alone to tend both the ailing baby and her social shame. "Maternity—Woman's Gethsemane" reads one of the intertitles that link Anna's plight with Jesus on the way to Calvary. As she realizes her infant son

Intolerance, 1916: Lillian Gish as the figure of Eternal Motherhood.

is dying, Anna pours a lifetime of devotion and desperation into her few moments of motherhood. Like Pickford's Tess, she baptizes the child (with the garishly ironic name Trust Lennox) and breathes on its cold hands in a futile fight to sustain its life. This is a performance of exquisitely balanced frenzy and subtlety; John Barrymore, the preeminent romantic classical actor of his day, called it "the most superlative exquisite and poignantly enchanting thing I have ever seen in my life."

Gish stayed with Griffith longer than his other top stars, leaving in 1921 for the company that would become Metro-Goldwyn-Mayer, where she continued to suffer triumphantly in *The White Sister, La Bohème* and *The Wind*. She was able to make **The Scarlet Letter** (1926) only after convincing balky Protestant groups that the Nathaniel Hawthorne novel, about a fiery Puritan minister who sires a child with a member of his congregation, would not give religious offense. Gish and Frances Marion, the eminent scenarist who wrote twenty Pickford films, solved or sidestepped this problem by focusing on Hester Prynne (Gish), not the Reverend Dimmesdale (Lars Hanson), and by making her another in the actress's long line of wronged women. Marked with a scarlet "A" for "adulteress," cursed and besmirched by the sanctimonious locals, Hester is every bit as unjustly ostracized as Anna was in *Way Down East*.

This time, the love child, Pearl, gets a proper baptism—from her father the reverend—and grows into healthy girlhood. Eight years after Pearl's birth, Hester wants to flee to Europe with her daughter and Dimmesdale; she tears off her embroidered "A" and removes her bonnet to let her long hair flow free as a signifier of her sexual liberation. But the minister must pay for his "sin." He denounces himself before the congregation, revealing an "A" branded on his chest. In one of many Pietà images in Gish films, he dies in Hester's arms, asking, "Is this not a better freedom than any we have dreamed of?" Well, no, but, under Victor Sjöström's acute directorial hand, the ending emphasizes the silent-film law that a lover's survival is less important than a mother's.

facing page: The Scarlet Letter, 1926: Lillian Gish as Hester Prynne, with Joyce Coad as her daughter, Pearl.

SACRIFICING IN SILENCE, AND SACRIFICING IN THE SILENTS

Less important, that is, unless the mother's death makes for better melodrama, as in that warhorse of self-sacrifice, *Madame Butterfly*. One version of that story, 1922's **The Toll of the Sea**, which Frances Marion adapted and Chester M. Franklin directed, was the first Technicolor feature shot in the U.S.—and the rare American silent film with a non-Caucasian female lead. Anna May Wong, born in Los Angeles's Chinatown, would later costar with Douglas Fairbanks (*The Thief of Bagdad*) and Marlene Dietrich (*Shanghai Express*). She was just seventeen when she played the Asian child-woman in love with a white man.

The sea throws Allen Carver (Kenneth Harlan) onto the rocks near a Chinese village, where he is rescued and cared for by young Lotus Flower (Wong). He leaves her with child and returns four years later with a Caucasian wife. Lotus Flower sees her duty and hands the child over to his new family, after which she throws herself into the sea that brought her a two-edged gift. The climax is the standard act of noble renunciation—bowing to convention while showing how it destroys decent people—that the movies frequently imposed on heroic outsiders. Wong, who cries real, fat tears when Lotus Flower is heartbroken, shares her most intense scene with the wonderfully poised child performer known as Baby Moran. Taken from his mother and held by Carver's wife, the little boy touches Wong's face, leans in and, with great tenderness, kisses her twice. A good child always knows its rightful mother.

So often, for the virgin goddesses of the silent cinema, the purest emotion was not between woman and man but mother and child. Greta Garbo usually played women of the world whose attachment to any man could be a kiss of death for him or her. A goddess from a distant, cooler planet, the Garbo woman rarely bothered to marry, let alone bear a child—because, in any screen affair, she was the far more mature one, a figurative mother to her callow courtiers. (Garbo's two films based on *Anna Karenina*, in which her Anna makes a rapturous connection with her young sons, are addressed in the "Perennial Moms" chapter.)

Imported from Sweden in 1925, after supporting roles in just three feature films,

The Toll of the Sea, 1922: Will Anna May Wong forfeit her child (Baby Moran) to his father's Caucasian wife (Beatrice Bentley)?

Garbo was a relative novice in movies. Yet she intuitively understood the unique power of silent-screen acting: how the fervid glance, the slumped shoulders or the gentle caressing of a child could express emotion as eloquently as any stirring oration. By 1926, with Pickford in *Sparrows*, Gish in *The Scarlet Letter* and Garbo at the beginning of her sixteen-year reign at MGM, Hollywood had refined the silent film into a unique and elevated art form. As Pickford dismissively said, "Adding sound to movies would be like putting lipstick on the Venus de Milo." In fact, the Warner brothers were about to apply exactly that cosmetic—giving rise to the talkies and, within three years, effectively slaughtering the silents.

The birth of talking pictures was long in gestation. As early as 1889, Edison and Dickson had devised a machine that could record sound with film. When the medium reached its early maturity in the years after *The Birth of a Nation*, silent films were rarely silent. Indeed, every movie was also a musical: in smaller houses a pianist seated to one side of the screen would accompany the images, and in the movie palaces a full orchestra performed elaborate pastiche scores. By the mid-twenties, technology had advanced to permit sound to be recorded on film (the system that would be used for the first eighty years of talkies) or

The Jazz Singer, 1927:
Al Jolson sings to his "mammy" (Eugenie Besserer).

on records played in sync with the drama. The Warners employed the latter process, known as Vitaphone, for ***The Jazz Singer***: the first feature film to include singing and some talking. Al Jolson's cry to the audience—"Wait a minute, wait a minute, you ain't heard nothin' yet!"—was truly the shout heard 'round the world.

Jolson, the Lithuanian rabbi's son known as the World's Greatest Entertainer, plays Jakie Rabinowitz, whose father the cantor (Warner Oland, the Swede who later impersonated Charlie Chan in sixteen movies) insists he go into the family business. He condemns the boy's love of Negro-inflected secular music, while Jakie's mother, Sara (Eugenie Besserer), encourages him to follow his heart and art. With this maternal blessing, Jakie changes his name to Jack Robin and becomes a vaudeville star. As Sara proudly says (in intertitles), "He's not *my* boy anymore—he belongs to the whole world now." Jakie returns briefly to the congregation, replacing his dying father to sing the "Kol Nidre." The cantor addresses his last words to his wife: "Mama, we have our son again." In the final scene, Jakie is back onstage, in blackface, belting the maternal torch song "My Mammy." "Doncha know me?" he cries out to a tearful, smiling Sara in the front row. "It's your little baby!"

Ladies and gentlemen, mothers and sons: the talkies!

The Sin of Madelon Claudet, 1931: Helen Hayes with Neil Hamilton, in the happy prelude to decades of suffering.

THE MOTHER MARTYRS OF PRE-CODE

Condemned by society or hounded by fate,
these mothers heroically protected
their children in the early Depression years.

The "Pre-Code era"—actually, the period between the introduction of a moderately liberal Production Code in 1930 and the establishment of a much stricter set of rules that went into effect July 1, 1934—is fondly recalled for saucy movies that spoke in the tart cadences of fast-talking men and faster women. This freedom created fresh stars, including James Cagney, Barbara Stanwyck, Mae West and Jean Harlow, and teased audiences with a sexual impudence that riled the burghers of propriety. Watch *Baby Face* or *Employees' Entrance* or *The Story of Temple Drake* and feel the sizzle.

In Hollywood movies and American life, though, other codes of behavior still applied: that a man could desert a pregnant woman, or terminate a marriage if the girl wasn't of his class, or, in the depths of the Great Depression, sell his wife's child to a rich couple. Under those strictures, a quartet of strong movie mothers dared to assert rights to their children, against all the odds that a patriarchal, puritanical society could stack against them. Spanning years, often decades, these Pre-Code weepies put mothers on-screen, and their avatars in the audience, through the emotional wringer. They may not have the contemporary sass of the Cagney films, but they can still touch hearts, because their themes of love and loss, sacrifice and redemption, are timeless.

"I wish Spaniards wouldn't put so much tragedy in their music," says the bon vivant Carlo (Lewis Stone) to his mistress Madelon (Helen Hayes) one night at the theater. "They ask for love with so many tears." Watching **The Sin of Madelon Claudet** in theaters in 1931, moviegoers shed buckets of tears at this portrayal of the purest love: Madelon's for Larry, the son she had to abandon soon after he was born. A French country girl who falls for an American painter (Neil Hamilton) and is left pregnant when he returns home, Madelon falls much farther: into a liaison with the cool Carlo, a jewel thief masquerading as a count; into a ten-year jail sentence, when Carlo is arrested and she convicted for his crimes; and onto the streets, where she is reduced to getting men drunk and stealing their money. And all in support of the son she has rarely seen. Put baldly, this is the story of a woman who becomes a prostitute to put her boy through med school. But can a harlot also be a saint? Kindly Dr. Dulac (Jean Hersholt) thinks so, saying of Madelon and Larry that her "life has been one long martyrdom for him."

Adapting Edward Knoblock's 1923 play *The Lullaby*, screenwriter Charles MacArthur (Hayes's husband) tightened the dramatic strings by dispensing with a murder trial, having Dr. Dulac narrate the story to Larry's wife and elevating the young man's vocation from sailor to physician, which affords him a professional as well as personal interest in the woman who crosses his path only twice. MacArthur also gave his wife, a Broadway star in her talking-film debut, a role to display the range of emotions that would win her a Best Actress Oscar. Hayes ages seamlessly from teen farm girl to courtesan to a pretty petty thief and then to an "old hag" whose company no man would pay for—and who, when an innkeeper reaches for her purse, screams, "Keep off of me or I'll cut your face open!" Yet in Hayes's performance, under Edgar Selwyn's acute direction, Madelon betrays no shame for her actions, no regret or self-pity for her sorry status. Money is life for this woman, because every penny she earns or steals goes to Dr. Dulac to support Larry's studies. "Tell him he had a good mother," she says to Dulac, who replies, "A great mother."

From Madelon's tragedy, Hayes makes plangent music. Her emotional arias come in four magnificent scenes:

1. When Madelon gives birth, she speaks in gaunt delirium: "I wish it was dead. I wish we were both dead. Take it away!" But when handed the baby, she becomes instantly attached and addicted to motherhood, smiling through tears at this social burden for her to endure, this gift for her to redeem.

2. In prison, she leans into the mesh screen separating her from her friend Rosalie (Marie Prevost), who has kept contact with the boy. Through the mesh, she kisses Rosalie once, then again, saying of the second kiss, "That was for him."

3. After her release from prison, Madelon meets Larry (Frankie Darro), now about thirteen and a ward of the state. He confesses that he fought with another boy who called his mother a jailbird—"'cause anybody as beautiful as my mother wouldn't be in jail." Identifying herself as someone who knew Madelon, and realizing that Larry's devotion for his missing mother is as innocent and intense as hers for him, she decides to protect the boy's reputation by telling him his mother is dead. Then she asks, "Could you give an old friend a kiss?" As he pecks her on the lips, she clasps his face in her

hands like a lifeline. As he leaves, she begs for a hug and devours him in her embrace. "That's from your mother."

4. In her only scene with the grown Larry (Robert Young), she has entered his home for one last meeting. Still without revealing her identity, she tells him that she is a mother who lost contact with her child. Larry diagnoses her physical condition as dire, adding, "I guess mothers are hard to kill." She holds his hands, gazing up with both a spaniel's adoration and a mother's pride in her caring son, then retreats into the night. Larry's wife (Karen Morley), to whom Dr. Dulac relates Madelon's story, says, "She should have told him." "Oh," Dulac says, "she's too great a woman for that." So everyone keeps the secret from Larry. Missing the big reconciliation is frustrating for audiences, but the moral must be: Where's the sanctity in maternal martyrdom if you brag about it?

"I'm taking the kid with me," reads the farewell note from the rotten, barely literate husband in the 1930 film *Sarah and Son*. "You're not a fit wife, and a woman who is not a fit wife isn't a fit mother, neither. He'll be all right, don worry. Better than with you. But you will never see I or him again." Sarah Storm (Ruth Chatterton), an Austrian immigrant who is the fittest wife and mother imaginable, has long wished for the departure of the shiftless, abusive Jim (Fuller Mellish Jr.), her partner in a vaudeville act. "Maybe I'd be sorry like nothing," she says. "I'd be glad to get rid of such a big loafer." He's gone soon enough, as malingering impregnators often are in Pre-Code weepies. But to abscond with their child is to rob Sarah of one of her two reasons for living: motherhood and show business. She also learns that her younger sister Rosel, whom she raised from infancy, has died back in Austria. As Sarah hones her singing skills and American accent by entertaining World War I troops in hospitals, she encounters Jim again, who speaks one word: "Ashmore"—the name of the Texas oil baron to whom, years before, he sold Bobby.

In ten more years, Sarah has become a "prima donna soprano" with enough for-

Sarah and Son, 1930: Ruth Chatterton fights for years to reclaim her son (Philippe De Lacy).

tune to engage lawyer Howard Vanning (Fredric March) to search for her son. Mrs. Ashmore (Doris Lloyd) refuses to allow Sarah a visit with the boy and, when she insists, spitefully sends an imposter— a deaf-mute. Finally meeting the real Bobby (Philippe De Lacy, Greta Garbo's son in the 1927 *Anna Karenina* adaptation *Love*) on a dock at Vanning's country home, Sarah befriends him and, on a boat ride, saves him from drowning. As Bobby lies in bed, delirious, both "mothers" enter. He cries out, "Mother! It's cold! I'm afraid"—and hugs Sarah. "He knows, somehow," the chastened Mrs. Ashmore acknowledges. And Sarah sings the tune with which she used to lull Bobby to sleep: Brahms's "Lullaby" (the theme of this movie, and of *The Sin of Madelon Claudet*). The boy has his mother and, with Vanning, perhaps a good father as well. Under Dorothy Arzner's direction, Chatterton—diva of the soulful, reproachful glance—wrestles her early *mittel*-European accent to a draw, and by the end nearly matches her work in 1929's *Madame X*. This time, the boy she loves gets to know who his mom is.

. . .

A wronged woman seeking reunion with her son needed twenty, twenty-five years to accomplish the job: that was the dictum that governed Madelon Claudet, Madame X, Sarah Storm and Ellen Holmes, whom Jean Arthur embodies in director Lambert Hillyer's *The Most Precious Thing in Life* (1934) as a sweet teen aging into spinsterhood. In their courtship at Eastmore College, the rich-boy football hero Bob Kelsey (Donald Cook) is keen on Ellen, who works in the college laundry, as her mother did. But once they're married and back home with his snooty mother (Mary Forbes), the difference in class clashes like cymbals or symbols. Ellen wants to call their new son Francis. "Such a common name," says the elder Mrs. K, and the boy is christened Christopher. When Bob insists on his mother raising the boy, Ellen leaves, and the Kelseys tell the child his mother is dead.

Fast-forward to 1930, when Ellen is now a washerwoman at Eastmore, which Chris (Richard Cromwell) has entered as a freshman. A pampered bully, as befits his upbringing, Chris needs an education—mothering—from the old woman he calls Biddy. She offers tips on how to impress the football coach (Ward Bond) and steers him toward pretty Patty O'Day (Anita Louise), a younger version of herself. When his father objects to Chris's romantic alliance with a splendid girl of the lower class, Ellen confronts him. "You want him to marry that scrubwoman's daughter?" he demands, leaving him defenseless against her zinger, "He's a scrubwoman's son." Now Ellen spits out the truth she so long withheld: "For twenty years I've kept still, so he could have what I thought was the best. Do you think I'm going to let you cheat him now? You've had your chance and you've ruined it. Now it's my turn. I'm not going to let you wreck my boy's happiness."

A few years before she became Frank Capra's all-American glamour girl in *Mr. Deeds Goes to Town*, *You Can't Take It with You* and *Mr. Smith Goes to Washington*, Arthur plays the elder Ellen, who's barely forty, in gray hair pulled back in a bun and with cobweb lines of age on her pallid face. (Hayes as Madelon Claudet achieved a similar makeunder.) Also, Arthur's honeyed voice assumes a high-pitched, wizened tone, like the Cumaean Sybil with strep throat. Her Ellen speaks with an authority she has earned in two decades of suffering at the soft hands of class prejudice, and all

The Most Precious Thing in Life, 1934: Jean Arthur as Biddy, whose son (Richard Cromwell) doesn't realize that his college-dorm cleaning lady is his mother.

to claim the most precious thing in life: a mother's right to guide her spoiled son into being a loving, responsible man.

Class differences become cultural chasms in *Madame Butterfly*, Paramount's 1932 adaptation of the John Luther Long story that David Belasco turned into a Broadway hit and Giacomo Puccini into an opera warhorse. Sylvia Sidney might seem an odd choice to play the high-born Japanese woman who marries an American navy officer and is left to cope with their child and hope for his return. Like Barbara Stanwyck, Sidney parlayed New York grit and gravity into a tantalizing screen glamour. Yet she brings pathos and humor to Cho-Cho San, who brags of her pidgin English, "I learned from a visiting scholar. She teach me very high-class Brooklyn accent." (Sidney was Bronx-born.) A preternaturally mature star by

Madame Butterfly, 1932: Sylvia Sidney as Cho-Cho San, from ancient Tokyo by way of the Bronx, with Cary Grant as Lieutenant Pinkerton.

the age of twenty, in the 1931 films *City Streets*, *Street Scene* and *An American Tragedy*, Sidney was dubbed "the Saddest Eyes in Hollywood"; her tears could sparkle like emeralds. She sheds a noble shower of them here, under Marion Gering's direction, and in the general direction of Cary Grant's Lieutenant Pinkerton. Simultaneously hoping and grieving, Sidney fills those eyes with the solemn, soaring music of a woman whose son is the only living remnant of a vanished love.

At the start, Cho-Cho San is already mourning a death: her mother's. "May I do nothing to bring dishonor to my departed mother's honorable name," she intones to her gods. "Make it possible for me to be of assistance to my illustrious family from now on, even though I'm only a woman." However subservient the words, Sidney stares heavenward like a haughty headmistress. Then, after she allows Pinkerton to court her, Cho-Cho San indirectly causes her father's suicide, being told, "Your father died with honor when he could no longer live with honor." Pinkerton weds her, in what he believes is a ceremony valid only in Japan, and sails away. "I will wait for always," Cho-Cho San avers. "I know he will come. He will not forget." She gives her child (played by Philip Horomato, the only Asian in the cast) the name Trouble, saying to the absent Pinkerton, "We wait till you come back to call him Joy." Butterfly sustains her wan hope for four years, until the lieutenant returns with his "real" (American) wife. After handing her child over to the couple, she follows her father into the afterlife by committing suicide.

Three women—Madelon, Sarah and Ellen—lose their children, then metaphorically reclaim them. One, Cho-Cho San, raises her son and gives him away. All four of these films' leading actresses locate every nugget of histrionic gold. Sidney especially brings a power, both demure and defiant, to the handover of her child. It is not a gesture of surrender but a gift from a goddess who sinned by loving a mortal. Her Butterfly is a deity who dies.

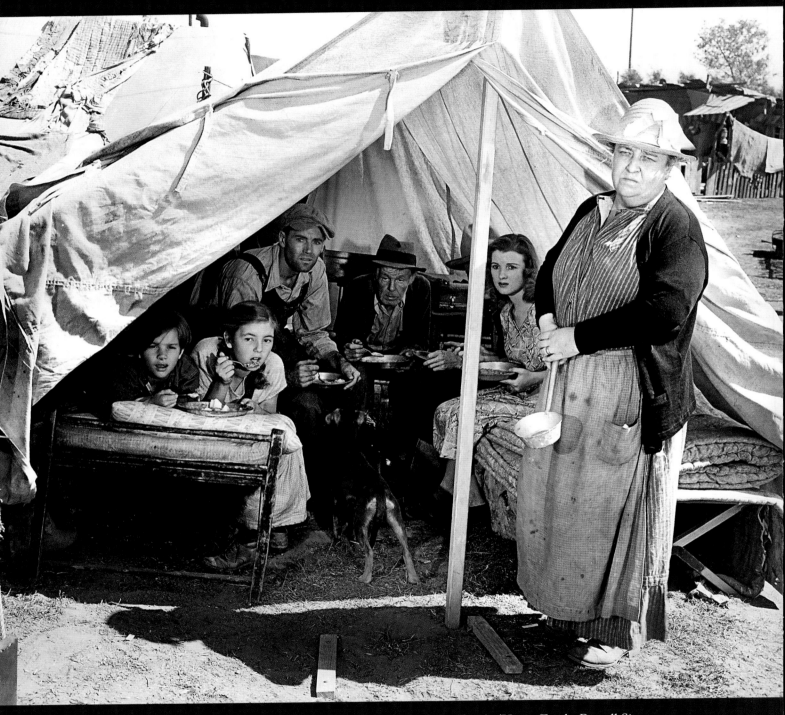

The Grapes of Wrath, 1940: Ma Joad (Jane Darwell) leads her family (Henry Fonda, Russell Simpson, Doris Bowdon seated in the rear) to California, the land of broken promises.

THE GREAT AMERICAN MOM

As warm and nourishing as apple pie.

They endured hardship in the silent films and in the early talkies, then flourished in the 1940s: the decade of the great American movie mom. Back when going to the pictures was a happy national habit—when, in 1946, 150 million Americans bought four *billion* movie tickets, or one every two weeks for every man, woman and child in the country—Hollywood made most of its product for the family and made sure Mom was part of the audience's on-screen family. Some of the most acclaimed and popular films of the forties portrayed the heroism of mothers. Poor women led their broods across the country for a better life, and Ma Joad was there in *The Grapes of Wrath*. Women whose husbands had gone to war sacrificed to maintain civility at home: Anne Hilton in *Since You Went Away* and Kay Miniver in *Mrs. Miniver*. Women used tact and music to restore harmony to the household: Mrs. Smith in *Meet Me in St. Louis*. Women struggled to raise their children above their own status: Katie Nolan *in A Tree Grows in Brooklyn* and Marta Hanson in *I Remember Mama.*

These and a hundred other female characters in forties films fused into the Great American Movie Mom. The sextet of moms in this chapter represents a small but instructive glimpse at how Hollywood made good films about good women. Ma Joad and Katie Nolan might hide their love under a veneer of toughness, but they believed their guiding mission was to elevate their offspring. And the other four lavished affection as their children's confessor, coach and cheerleader. Call them the tip of the nice-berg.

The Joad family in *The Grapes of Wrath* (1940) ought to be called Job, so many plagues do they suffer. In the Oklahoma dust bowl, the sharecroppers forfeit their land and their home, which Ma Joad (Jane Darwell) is ready to leave without a farewell glance: "I never had my house pushed over before. Never had my family stuck out on the road. Never had to lose everything I had in life." The sprawling family crowds into an old truck to seek an employment bonanza promised in California. Isn't it the Golden State? But both grandparents die en route. The child of Ma's daughter Rose of Sharon is stillborn. The family can earn only five cents a box for picked peaches, and the farm they work is effectively a prison, with barbed wire and armed guards. Son Tom (Henry Fonda) gets involved in labor agitation and kills a man. Directed by John Ford and scripted by Nunnally Johnson from John Steinbeck's novel, the movie wrings every drop of rage and pathos out of the plight of desperate farmers, ten years into the Depression.

Tom is the firebrand of the family, Ma the hearth. She sees the Joads' woes as the middle chapter in a story as old as humankind. "Woman can change better than a man," she says. "A man lives sorta, well, in jerks. Baby's born or somebody dies, and that's a jerk. He gets a farm or loses it, and that's a jerk. With a woman, it's all in one flow, like a stream. Little eddies and waterfalls. But the river, it goes right on." She might be describing the difference between male- and female-oriented Hollywood films, between combustion and continuity. In the movie's famous peroration, Ma proclaims that the underclass will triumph because women like her have the power to replenish America with their children, millions of them. "Rich fellas come up and they die," she says, "and their kids ain't no good and *they* die out. But we keep a-comin'. We're the people that live. They can't wipe us out; they can't lick us. We'll go on forever, Pa, 'cause we're the people." As men kill, so women give life. Their bodies are the arsenals of future generations.

Ma Joad is on the front lines of a labor battle. Anne Hilton (Claudette Colbert) in **Since You Went Away** (1944) mans—or womans—the home front when her husband goes to war. Producer David O. Selznick's metaphorical follow-up to *Gone With the Wind*, with World War II replacing the Civil War, again ignores the men risking their lives in the field to concentrate on the women coping without them. But unlike Scarlett O'Hara, whose ambition drove her into business to save her plantation, Anne exhibits the more passive heroism of waiting and worrying, her smile a rictus of dread, her poise a plug for the scream lodged in her heart.

In this nearly three-hour movie, the drama comes in the silence that may be punctuated at any moment by a phone call, or the doorbell ring of a Western Union telegram, announcing a death in the family. Anne's two daughters—college-age Jane (Jennifer Jones) and teenage Bridget (Shirley Temple)—try pursuing the adventures of girls their age; they also volunteer for the war effort, as does Anne eventually, by working in a shipyard. The Hiltons do nothing so indecorous as suffer; they abide and endure. Only Jones, under John Cromwell's direction, gets to emote in sync with women in the audience whose beaux never came home. And to both parental roles, Anne must add that of chaplain, when she comforts Jane by urging catharsis: "Cry, darling. Cry your heart out. I won't try to tell you that you'll get over it soon, because it will take time. Maybe a long time."

· · ·

Since You Went Away, 1944: Jennifer Jones (left) and Shirley Temple listen as mother Claudette Colbert reads a letter from their father away at war.

Greer Garson in **Mrs. Miniver** (1942) had something to cry about. World War II left English cities, and Kay Miniver's decorous village of Balham, cratered by Nazi bomb raids; the local church lost its roof in those sorties. She suffers the loss of family; she confronts and disarms a downed German aviator. She is determined to maintain a semblance of normality by reading her youngest son *Alice in Wonderland* during an air raid. Mrs. Miniver taught that there's no crying in wartime, except in the audience. She kept a stiff upper lip even as moviegoers' lips were tremulous from her shining example.

The United States was never in danger of Nazi planes strafing its cities, but American boys were risking their lives in the European Theater. The movie meant to show what they were fighting for; as film historian David Thomson has written, it "conditioned American public opinion to the sentimental explanation for a necessary war." Directed by William Wyler at MGM's Culver City studios, the movie featured Canadian Walter Pidgeon as husband Clem and New Yorkers Richard Ney and Teresa Wright as their grown son and his wife. (Not long after the filming, Garson the mother married Ney the son.) Studio boss Louis B. Mayer made sure that the Minivers approximated his ideal of small-town Americana, but with a starchier accent; Andrew Sarris called the Minivers a "British version of the Hardy family." Because Kay Miniver is Yankee by adoption and adaptation, she qualifies as a Great American Mom.

Out of twelve Oscar nominations, *Mrs. Miniver* won six: Best Picture, Director, Actress (Garson), Supporting Actress (Wright), Screenplay and Black and White Cinematography. Everyone loved the movie; Winston Churchill called it "propaganda worth a hundred battleships," and Nazi propaganda minister Joseph Goebbels urged the German film industry to study and imitate it. Churchill was speaking from gratitude, Goebbels from envy—and all at a mother's resolve to celebrate the small gifts of life as the skies rain death.

Forties films could create dramatic sparks without resorting to political outrage or the background noise of the war against Hitler. Mothers didn't have to domineer and dominate to be persuasive. Sometimes a woman's gentlest

Mrs. Miniver, 1942: Greer Garson and Walter Pidgeon clutch their children
(Christopher Severn and Clare Sanders) during an air raid.

touch could push her husband's buttons and coax him toward the decision that she and her children hoped for. A single subtle scene can reveal it. In ***Meet Me in St. Louis*** (1944), set in December 1903 in MGM's dream of the urban Midwest, businessman Alonzo Smith (Leon Ames) has been offered a better job in New York. His announcement of the family's imminent departure triggers heartache and resentment for his girls, Rose (Lucille Bremer), Esther (Judy Garland), Agnes (Joan Carroll) and Tootie (Margaret O'Brien), who bolt from the dinner table to their rooms. Only his wife, Anna (Mary Astor), remains, attending his sputtering with a gaze that scrupulously avoids reproach. Following him into the living room and handing him his cake, she says gravely, "If you think it's best for us to go away, why, that's what we'll do."

She sits down at the piano to play the love ballad "You and I" (cowritten by the film's producer, Arthur Freed). "It's good to hear you play, Anna," Mr. Smith muses. "It's been a long time." When he tries singing in a scratchy tenor, his accompanist

Meet Me in St. Louis, 1944: Mary Astor and husband, Leon Ames, sing a song at Christmas, attended by daughter Margaret O'Brien.

obliges: "I'll put it down in your key." She prompts a few words, then sings in harmony. The four girls creep downstairs, eat their cake and listen to the last verse: "Time goes by, but we'll be together, you and I." Accompanying these musical sentiments of lasting love, director Vincente Minnelli's tableau of father, mother and daughters establishes that the clan will not crack, because who they are is more important than where they are. Anna's ostensible compromises, indicated by Astor with not even a secret smile, have secured the notion of a permanent home. The genius of motherhood has restored the family.

Some mothers get outshone by their husbands, at least in their children's eyes. That is the burden that Katie Nolan (Dorothy McGuire) finds most difficult to bear in *A Tree Grows in Brooklyn* (1945). She works tirelessly scrubbing floors to keep her singing-waiter husband Johnny (James Dunn, who won the Supporting Actor Oscar for the role) and their preteen children Francie (Peggy Ann Garner) and Neeley (Ted Donaldson) in their turn-of-the-century tenement flat. Yet Francie, the soul and narrator of director Elia Kazan's beautiful debut film, loves her irresponsible father as a vital force, while only tolerating her mother as the family's grim judge and drudge. Johnny provides the entertainment and Katie the essentials, which she thinks he and the kids take for granted; they appreciate his gaiety, not her utility. No one feels better knowing that Katie's hard work pays the rent; but when Johnny sings "Annie Laurie," even Katie's adamantine heart can soften. It reminds her of a million years ago, when she was young and in love with him. Since they had children they have grown into two mismatched boarders in the same apartment: Johnny the alcoholic charmer, Katie weary and severe. He can't quit drinking and she can't get bubbly.

Francie has the aspirations and aptitude to become a writer. (She grew up to become Betty Smith, whose memories of her Brooklyn family became the bestseller the movie was based on.) A helpful teacher asks her to understand the difference between imagination and pipe dreams, but for most of the film Francie's guiding pipe dream is her father. And because a child has to take sides, she views her mother with resentment, for not being Johnny. "Some of its best scenes," wrote *Time* critic James

A Tree Grows in Brooklyn, 1945: Dorothy McGuire (center)
with Peggy Ann Garner and Ted Donaldson.

Agee when the movie was released, "are those in which the long-estranged parents try vainly to make up, and in which the father and daughter realize, beyond any chance of forgetting, that she is growing up and that he never will." *A Tree Grows in Brooklyn* traces the growing up of both Katie, who realizes that Johnny's blarney is a healing gift, and Francie, who learns to like and love her mother. McGuire, who was often cast as an ideal mom in Disney films (*Old Yeller*, *Swiss Family Robinson*) and was Jesus's mother in *The Greatest Story Ever Told*, finds the perfect register for Katie, a woman who can't express the devotion she feels for her dear, bright daughter. Katie is a mother whose mute heroism only the sympathetic viewer can see.

Marta Hanson (Irene Dunne) in ***I Remember Mama*** (1948) is a secular saint, worth praying to for special favors—because she always gives. Like the Sally Benson book that spawned *Meet Me in St. Louis*, and

I Remember Mama, 1948: Irene Dunne as the Northern nurturer who lovingly provides the best for her family, including daughter Katrin (Barbara Bel Geddes, far right).

Smith's *A Tree Grows in Brooklyn*, Kathryn Forbes's *Mama's Bank Account* was a fictionalized memoir, this one looking back in rapture at her Norwegian mother's grit and gentility. Kindness seeps through Marta's formal manner as she does the weekly accounts, adjudicates among her three contentious sisters, and scrimps to educate her four children. The one boy, Nels (Steve Brown), wants to attend high school; at Mama's urging, the three daughters chip in from their meager savings. Katrin (Barbara Bel Geddes), the story's narrator and rememberer, has literary dreams that she achieves with the publication of the lightly fictionalized story that became *Mama's Bank Account*. Mama, so industrious that her one nervous tic is to scrub the floor, impersonates a hospital cleaning woman to sneak in to see her youngest daughter. Other than that, sensational incidents are few.

This may seem an impossibly idealized family portrait, yet the film, directed by George Stevens, provides an acute, organic view of the Hanson home—its ebb and flow, as Ma Joad might call it. So chipper is the mood of the piece that, when it ran for nearly two years on Broadway (where Nels was played by the young Marlon Brando), it was described as a comedy. Dunne often brought a coloratura comic lilt to her films. That larkish impulse is subdued here, in a movie role first offered to Greta Garbo, but Dunne's Marta is reserved, not grave. (And her resemblance to Bel Geddes, in their soft, rhyming faces, makes them look not just kindred but kin.) Her generous spirit sets a high standard for the other family members; it lifts them to meet her. An extraordinary ordinary woman, Marta is a nexus of maternal virtues: the great Norwegian-American mom.

On Jane Darwell in
The Grapes of Wrath

Being an actress, wife, mother and grandmother has been the best of all worlds for me. All these roles have given me an understanding of what it means to have close and important family relationships.

This kind of family love and devotion was beautifully depicted in the 1940 John Ford film *The Grapes of Wrath*, based on the novel by John Steinbeck. It's the story of a poor sharecropper family making its way west in the 1930s, looking for work. They journey from the dust bowl of Oklahoma to California in a broken-down truck during the Great Depression.

The actress Jane Darwell plays the mother who keeps the family all together. She's a devoted wife, mother and grandmother who cleans, washes and cooks without a break; she's everything to everyone in the family. There's not one false moment in her performance, a magnificent portrayal of a true farm lady who loves and is devoted to her family. In a wrenching good-bye scene, she knows one of her sons (played by Henry Fonda) must leave the family and sends him off with all her love. Of course, her heart is breaking, but she'll cry after he leaves.

These are life lessons to be learned and Jane Darwell was a fine teacher. I saw *The Grapes of Wrath* in the late fifties, when I was a young mother, and it made a lasting and indelible impression on me. Inspired by Darwell's closeness to her family, I turned down several films because I didn't want to be away from home, and I chose to take our children with me on two distant film shoots that didn't interfere with their schooling: *Exodus* and *Grand Prix*. I admired Darwell's combination of tenderness and strength, and she became a role model for me.

There's no better example of motherhood in a film that I have ever seen. It's no wonder she won an Academy Award for her performance. The picture was made in 1940, but Darwell's beautiful portrayal lives on.

—*Eva Marie Saint*

A Hardy clan: Fay Holden as Emily Hardy shares a laugh with Mickey Rooney as Andy.

SERIAL MOMS

The wife-mother flourished in family-friendly film series.

The movie landscape was so different, almost lunar, before the James Bond films legitimized big-budget sequels in the 1960s. Since then, the sequel has become the norm. In nine of the past ten years, the top-grossing picture has been an extension of some earlier blockbuster. (The one exception: *Avatar*.) Pre-Bond, though, the most successful Hollywood movies were unique and induplicable; nobody made a *Gone With the Wind II* or *The Even Better Years of Our Lives*. In the 1940s, the only sequels to be among their years' ten most popular films were four of the Bob Hope–Bing Crosby *Road* movies, *The Bells of St. Mary's* (with Bing reprising his Father Chuck O'Malley character from *Going My Way*) and *Jolson Sings Again* (following *The Jolson Story*).

Far below these, in budget and popular esteem, were the family-films series: thrifty B movies designed to fill the bottom half of a studio's double-feature bill. In these modest, amiable entertainments, such wife-mother types as Louise Jones, Blondie Bumstead and Phoebe Kettle flourished or at least persisted from the mid-1930s to the mid-'50s. They sketched the domestic grit of the middle- or working-class woman coping with the comic shortcomings of her kin. Her motto: not divide and conquer, but abide and endure.

These movies have to be distinguished from the postwar "A" film series *Father of the Bride* and *Father's Little Dividend* (with Joan Bennett and Spencer Tracy as the parents) and *Cheaper By the Dozen* and *Belles on Their Toes* (with Myrna Loy and Clifton Webb), each of which lasted only two episodes. The Jones family, *Blondie* and *Ma and Pa Kettle* pictures stretched over seventeen, twenty-eight and ten features, re-spectively. They also focused far more acutely on the burden of motherhood than did MGM's two "family" series of higher esteem: **The Thin Man** and the **Hardys**. Nick and Nora Charles (William Powell and Myrna Loy) suaved their way through six MGM features from 1934 to 1947—a fantasy of the chic married couple beloved by swells and thugs alike. By the fourth entry, *Shadow of the Thin Man*, they had acquired a son, Nick Jr. (Dickie Hall), who had sprouted into a teenager (Dean Stockwell) by the 1947 finale, *Song of the Thin Man*, but little Nicky was a less prominent and useful member of the clan than the Charles's wire fox terrier, Asta.

And though the fifteen Hardy films from 1937 to 1946 surely fit MGM boss Louis B. Mayer's dewy vision of the American family, the moral authority on view was utterly patriarchal. In nearly every episode, impulsive Andy (Mickey Rooney) would commit some minor breach of propriety, think himself a big shot in small-town Carvel, and receive a third-act lesson from his father, Judge James Hardy (Lewis Stone); his study is Andy's courtroom. And the judge takes his counsel less from his wife, Emily (Fay Holden), than from maiden aunt Milly (Sara Haden).

Emily would disappear for a film to tend her ailing mother, and in *Judge Hardy and Son* she risks death from pneumonia—not giving care but needing it. Andy relies on his mom for favors, his father for wisdom. The route of sagacity is more man-to-boy than mother-to-child. Sister Marian (Cecilia Parker) might get maternal advice from Emily, but since the stories depended on Andy's mischief, and the series on Rooney's star quality, girl talk was mostly a background whisper.

The *Jones Family* series, at 20th Century-Fox, preceded the MGM Hardys by a year: the first installment, 1936's *Every Saturday Night* (in which the family name was Evers), launched a seasonal skein, four films a year, until *On Their Own* concluded the project in 1940. In small-town Maryville, pharmacist John Jones (Jed Prouty) and his wife, Louise (Spring Byington, who played Andy's mom in the first Hardy film, *A Family Affair*), share a crowded home with their five children—sensible eldest daughter Bonnie (Shirley Deane), egotistical Jack (Kenneth Howell), studious Roger (George Ernest), histrionic Lucy (June Carlson) and baby Bobby (Billy Mahan)—and John's mother (Florence Roberts). In the sixth installment, *Hot Water*, John runs for Maryville mayor and wins. In the next film, *Borrowing Trouble*, John becomes a Big Brother to the orphan Tommy McGuire (Marvin Stephens), who moves in with the Joneses for the rest of the series. Occasionally the family travels: *Off to the Races, Down on the Farm, A Trip to Paris, The Jones Family in Hollywood*.

On the road or at home, the family dynamic rarely varies. John blusters as his children challenge the authority he tries to assert. Louise (billed in the screen credits as "Mrs. John Jones") knits and purrs, defusing family feuds with a smiling "Yes, dear" that could signal either approval or mild exasperation. The emotional anchor of the series, she also urges financial restraint in a money-strapped household with many mouths to feed; the Great Depression, still endemic, was the unspoken subtext in many Jones movies. But she frequently allows Granny—more tolerant of the kids than John, and more assertive than Louise—to fire the salvos of flinty common sense. "You're not bringing them up," Granny warns her son of his children in the first film, "you're always knocking them down." In the Jones family, it was often Grandmother who knew best.

The Jones Family films: parents Spring Byington and Jed Prouty at the
table with his mother (Florence Roberts) and the sprawling clan.

Barely nosed out in family-film obscurity by the 1938–41 Republic Pictures series
The Higgins Family (starring real-life husband, wife and son James, Lucile and Russell Gleason as the nuclear unit), the Joneses got little respect even from their own
studio. A 1936 Fox pressbook described the films as "energetic hokum . . . tolerably
amusing in an entirely inconsequential way . . . They strive, and rather successfully,
to catch the spirit of a small-town tribe; but that, in itself, is not too important an
enterprise." Important, perhaps not; salutary, for sure. The Jones movies allotted sympathy to every one of the family members, including Father; over the series they all
got to step out of their mild caricatures to reveal a clever brain and a giving heart. In
a film frame that could be clogged with eight or more Joneses fighting for attention,
the noise could be antiphonal but the lilting melody rang through—a chorus of all
for one and one for all.

*   *   *

A daily comic strip from 1930 to today—and over the decades a radio show, live-action TV sitcom and two animated cartoon specials—***Blondie*** came to movies in 1938. In the early days of Chic Young's strip, Blondie Boop-adoop had been a ditsy flapper and her beau Dagwood Bumstead a scion of wealth whose father disinherited him when he married. By the time of the Columbia film series, Blondie (Penny Singleton) had matured into an ideal of the American wife-mother: pert, sweet-tempered and ferociously competent—qualities needed to manage the household on a tight budget, and to save her amiably inept spouse (Arthur Lake) from catastrophes at home and at work with his splenetic boss J. C. Dithers (Jonathan Hale). Film historian Jeanine Basinger synopsized each plot of the series this way: "Dagwood screws everything up, and Blondie sorts everything out."

Given the youthful demands of their boy, Alexander, a.k.a. Baby Dumpling (Larry Simms), and their daughter, Cookie (Marjorie Ann Mutchie), who joined the family in 1942 in *Blondie's Blessed Event*, Blondie can be seen as a single mom with three kids. Dagwood is the perpetually addled adolescent, the good-hearted but hopeless teenage son whose appetites don't extend much beyond devouring the triple-decker sandwich that popular culture named after him. In the series debut, *Blondie!*, when Dagwood asks about the dinner menu, Blondie parries, "What difference does it make? You cover everything with ketchup anyway." In an argument, the two parents use the three-year-old Baby Dumpling as a marriage mediator; Blondie tells the child, "He forgets that we have a happy home because *I* planned and schemed." Dragged into court at the film's climax, she explains to the judge, "Most men have a lot of little boy in them." She turns the Bumstead bumbling into triumph when she wheedles a raise and a bonus out of Mr. Dithers for Dagwood. (In later films, Dithers will directly employ Blondie for the more complex deals.) Her last words: "Sometimes I think it's harder to raise a husband than a baby."

Lest Blondie come across as a scold, her tongue sharpened by domestic misery, Singleton delivers her lines with generous cheer. On Broadway from her teens as an eccentric dancer (under the name Dorothy McNulty) and in movies since 1930, when she led her college classmates through the rousing "Varsity Drag" in MGM's musical *Good News*, and much later the voice of space-age wife Jane on the cartoon series *The Jetsons*, Singleton radiated an unquenchable effervescence—think Ginger Rogers, cubed—and a good wife's tolerance for her husband's failings and flailings. She provided the perfect partner for Lake, a kind of Fred MacMurray lite, who softened Dagwood's doltishness with his blithely befuddled innocence. Though they endured a brief marital separation in 1939's *Blondie Meets the Boss* (she got custody of Baby Dumpling, Dagwood of the Bumstead dog, Daisy), the two loved and sustained each other; they and their children grew up together. The final film, *Beware of Blondie* in 1950, opens with a placid living room tableau: Mother knitting, Father reading, the teenage Alexander doing homework and grade-schooler Cookie playing the piano. The girl pauses in her practice to glance at her older brother's math problem and correct it. In the Bumstead family, heredity and Hollywood gave the girls all the brains.

Ma and Pa Kettle were real people—anyway, real*ish*. Neighbors of Betty MacDonald when she and her husband moved to Cape Flattery on Washington's Olympic Peninsula to become chicken farmers, the "Kettles" provided rural color to MacDonald's bestselling 1945 memoir *The Egg and I.* They also graced the 1947 movie version, starring Claudette Colbert and Fred MacMurray as the MacDonalds, and stole the show with their raucous backwoods wit. Recognizing the star quality of this supporting couple, Universal International gave the Kettles their own franchise, which lasted nine films, from 1949 to 1957.

As played by Marjorie Main (fifty-nine at the start of the series) and Percy Kilbride (sixty-one), Phoebe and Franklin Kettle might seem unlikely parents of fifteen kids who ranged from college age to infancy, but probability was the least of the screenwriters' concerns. This was flat-out, deadpan farce: a live-action cartoo of rubes who managed to survive with gumption and luck—and the popular success of their low-budget series. Each episode cost about $500,000 to produce and usually earned five times that amount at the box office. The guess here is that the peninsular couple who inspired the Ma and Pa characters never saw a penny of that largesse.

That scruple aside, as well as the derisive portrayal of two Native Americans (Oliver Blake and Teddy Hart) who helped out on the farm, the Ma and Pa films provide a lot of fun, in their oddly abrasive way. Though natives of the Pacific Northwest, the Kettles exhibit an inbred indolence that would be at home in Faulkner's Yoknapatawpha County, Mississippi. Ma, in a sack dress that Tyler Perry's Madea would consider *infra dig*, presides over a brood so large that she often refers to her kids by the wrong names. ("Now hang on there, Billy." "I'm Danny!") Ma's dinner table is a pigsty with plates, and her kitchen closet holds more junk than a full season of *Storage Wars;* "Might as well be one place as another," she opines. Pa, with a lower IQ than Ma's and a longer fuse, is a man of few words—his prayer before dinner is "Much obliged"—and compact actions: he changes radio stations by slamming his chair onto the floor. With children running around like field mice, Pa hardly gets the chance to relieve himself, drawling, "Maybe we should have had less kids and more bathrooms."

In the series debut, *Ma and Pa Kettle*, Pa wins a model home that promptly becomes a horror house. Then the Kettles get infected with wanderlust, in . . . *at the Fair, . . . on Vacation, . . . at Waikiki*, and . . . *in the Ozarks*. But with the whole family along, only the backdrop changes; the constant is Ma's gruffly doting, mostly unruffleable attitude toward her children. A few of the older kids are housebroken, but the rest seem feral. The "Be-ware of childrun" sign outside the farmhouse is no idle admonition: trespassers will be discouraged with slingshot rocks and peashooter pellets. In fact, the whole family is heavily armed. Suspicious of any stranger, they could be the Kettle militia, the Minute-Mas.

What's the appeal of these movies about a backwoods, backward family of borderline sociopaths? That the Kettles are presented without explanation or apology; they barge onto the screen, occupy it for an hour or so, then retreat until the next incursion, leaving the viewer to decide if they're nice, nuts or both. Sometimes they seem like yokel geniuses, as in . . . *Back on the Farm*'s classic scene of Ma and Pa "proving" on a blackboard that twenty-five divided by five is fourteen. (Watch it on YouTube: "Ma and Pa Kettle Math.") The Kettle films are the low-rent equivalents of

The Ma and Pa Kettle films: Marjorie Main and Percy Kilbride rode
herd on their fourteen, fifteen (nobody knew how many) kids.

those amazingly cluttered Preston Sturges comedies—*The Miracle of Morgan's Creek*
or *Hail the Conquering Hero*—except that the supporting cast of small-town eccen-
trics has seized control of the narrative. Kilbride, channeling the comic solemnity of
Buster Keaton, serves as the ideal opposite to Main, with her Brillo-pad voice and
hulking bonhomie; together they exhibited a kind of bleak hope on an endless road,
as if Vladimir and Estragon, in Samuel Beckett's *Waiting for Godot*, had been a married couple. Marjorie's Ma didn't have to lavish maternal sagacity on the kids, just
a kind of authority by default. Besides, they were all fellow lifers in the only prison
they knew and accepted: the Kettle family.

·　·　·

The B movie family series insisted not only on a continuity of talent (the actors were under contract) but continuity in writers and directors. If the *Blondie* series had auteurs, they would be Frank R. Strayer, director of the first dozen features, and Richard Flournoy, who wrote nine of those twelve. Charles Lamont helmed *Ma and Pa Kettle* and four of the eight sequels. Often, the craftsmen of one series moved on to others. Strayer came to *Blondie* after directing four of the Jones films. Karen DeWolf contributed scripts to both series. Jack Henley wrote six of the later Blondie movies, then four of the Kettles. These anonymous artisans probably considered this work not an adventure but a job: maneuvering stock domestic characters from Point A to Point B and back home again for supper.

For unlike the majority of golden age movies that pursued one story to its conclusion, but quite like the sitcoms then on radio and later on television, these family-film series didn't so much resolve as organically evolve: parents got older and children grew up. Andy Hardy graduated from high school, entered college and, in World War II, joined the military; in a 1958 postscript to the series, *Andy Hardy Comes Home*, he returned to Carvel with a family of his own. The movies' Blondie and Dagwood welcomed their second child, daughter Cookie, shortly after she was introduced in the comic strip. The Kettles' eldest son, Tom (Richard Long), studied animal husbandry at college and married the newspaper gal (Meg Randall) who had reported on the model home won by Ma and Pa. And when Bonnie Jones married her beau Herbert Thompson (*The Higgins Family*'s Russell Gleason), the family expanded to four generations, with episodes on newlywed economics (*Love on a Budget*) and the perils of young motherhood under the gaze of a buttinsky brood (*Everybody's Baby*). By the end of the series, three tiers of mothers—Grandma, Louise and Bonnie—were speaking womanly truth to male power, more or less simultaneously.

Aging with their audiences, encountering minor domestic trials and triumphs, the Joneses and the other film families came as close to a middle-class audience's rosy doubles as fictional characters could get. And since they showed up in new films three or four times a year, they might have been more familiar to a moviegoing woman than some of her own relatives. They were Ma, Pa and the rest of us kids, on the big screen.

Madame X, 1929: Young lawyer Raymond Hackett defends the mystery lady
Ruth Chatterton, who is—had he but known!—his mother.

PERENNIAL
MOMS

Mother stories retold across the decades.

On the stage, actresses test their mettle by playing a Shakespeare or Ibsen heroine, Blanche DuBois or Edward Albee's Martha. On-screen, classic novels may give birth to enduring female icons, as Leo Tolstoy's *Anna Karenina* has done for more than a century, but often the source is a French melodrama (*Madame X*) or the less elevated species of literature known as women's fiction (for *Stella Dallas* and *Imitation of Life*).

Whatever the provenance, these stories paint indelible portraits of women stigmatized by the sin of adultery, or by the accident of class or race. They lash loving mothers to the rack of noble suffering. And they reach their apogee with some form of convulsive public event: a trial, a wedding, a funeral or a train-station suicide. Crucially, these properties allow prominent stars to tear a passion to tatters. Here you will find Ruth Chatterton, Barbara Stanwyck, Greta Garbo, Vivien Leigh, Lana Turner (twice) and two other actresses—Fredi Washington and Susan Kohner—whose daring performances place them in that august company. That's a bonus of movies about Perennial Moms: they transcend stereotype to achieve archetype.

MADAME X

Alexandre Bisson's play, first staged in Paris in 1908, spread around the world like news of a royal scandal. In 1910 Broadway mounted two productions, one in French starring Sarah Bernhardt. The same year, the first movie version appeared in Denmark. Pauline Frederick headed a Hollywood silent feature adaptation in 1920, but talkies were the true medium for *Madame X*: all that suffering meted out to the hapless Jacqueline Floriot deserves to be declaimed rather than mimed. In all, Bisson's play spawned about a dozen screen versions, including an overwrought, undernourished 1966 version with Lana Turner and a more crackling 1981 TV movie starring Tuesday Weld.

The plot traces a woman's journey of degeneration and regeneration, sin and redemption. When Jacqueline commits adultery, her husband, a distinguished judge, bans her from their house and severs her ties to her beloved infant son Raymond, whom he tells that his mother is dead. As if to prove her husband's dim view of her actions, she leaves Paris and sinks into sin as the globe-trotting Madame X. Decades later, a drunken Jacqueline lets her real identity slip to the bounder Laroque. He takes her back to Paris, with plans to blackmail the judge, and she shoots him dead. When she goes on trial for murder, the young lawyer assigned to defend her is . . . Raymond! He doesn't know she is his mother, and she won't tell him.

The 1929 **Madame X**, directed by Lionel Barrymore, snagged a nomination for Best Actress in the second year of the Academy Awards and launched Ruth

Chatterton on a triumphant four-year run of movie agony at MGM and Warner Bros. All well earned, since she hits the proper high notes of emotion—full, not shrill—in each of Jacqueline's three big scenes. At the beginning, when her husband (Lewis Stone) exiles her from their home, she plants herself against the door she will vanish through and utters a sibylline curse. "Remember this," she intones, "that if it ever occurs to you again to tell that boy his mother is dead, you tell him too that her last request was to be allowed to look at him, just once. And you refused it. You tell him that, Louis." In her act 2 confrontation with the venomous Laroque (Ullrich Haupt), Chatterton's Jacqueline proves her maternal mettle by shooting him dead; the pain and resolution play subtly, starkly, across her face.

The climax, in which Jacqueline takes the witness stand to justify the killing of Laroque as the act of shielding her son from learning what his mother had become, propels Raymond (Raymond Hackett) into spasms of sympathy for her and denunciations of the unjust husband who sent her away—his own father, had he but known. Why is this mother's sacrifice kept secret, when every rule of melodrama screams for revelation, forgiveness and reconciliation? Perhaps because Jacqueline, having sinned and confessed, must pay her penance: saving her son's good name while denying herself a final healing embrace. The harboring of her secret makes Chatterton a screen sister to Helen Hayes in *The Sin of Madelon Claudet* and Jean Arthur in *The Most Precious Thing in Life*.

The 1937 **Madame X**, directed by Sam Wood, executes a few plot handsprings to satisfy a stricter Production Code and tilt some sympathy toward the husband. At the start, Jacqueline (Gladys George) is involved in a tryst that leads to a crime of passion. She returns home and finds that her son, Raymond, is ill; because she has evaded her duties as a mother and a wife, her husband Bernard (Warren William) is almost justified in throwing her out and in telling their son that his mother is dead. To hide from the law, she becomes a governess, not a harlot, while Bernard shows signs of kindness by searching for her. The climax is the same, with Jacqueline choosing death before her son's dishonor and the grown Raymond (John Beal) defending her as passionately as if he knows she is his own mother. "She was a wonderful woman, Father," he says at the end. "Whoever she was."

In the eight years between the 1929 and 1937 *Madame X* films, between the birth of talkies and their luxurious flowering, Hollywood had imposed a more natu-ralistic style of acting on sound films; George doesn't scale the histrionic Alps that Chatterton did, and the makeup that aged each actress twenty years is more nuanced here. But both performances are splendid, just in different registers—the difference between George's *sotto voce* and Chatterton's *fortissima*.

STELLA DALLAS

In some venerable films about sacrificing mothers, a murder can be easier to forgive than bad manners. And any poor woman deserves a rich husband, unless her demeanor and couture are loud enough to wake the neighbors—and embarrass her dear daughter. The 1923 novel *Stella Dallas* by Olive Higgins Prouty, who also wrote *Now, Voyager*, sees issues of class (upper vs. lower) as matters of tone in speaking (dulcet vs. braying) and dress. The gulf of social acceptance is nearly as wide as that between a black woman and a woman who can pass for white in the 1934 film *Imitation of Life*. Of course, a semblance of breeding is more easily achieved than a modification in skin color. If Henry Higgins had taught Stella Dallas the fine points of elocution, as he did for Eliza Doolittle, she might have kept her high-born husband, Stephen, and lived comfort-ably ever after. But then she would not have created a dilemma for her sweet Laurel: to choose between a birth mother and, as society and even Stella see it, a better one.

People who have never read *Stella Dallas*, or seen any of the films, know the ending: a mother standing in the rain, smiling through tears, as she peers into a townhouse window to glimpse her daughter's wedding. Here's the rest of the story. In a weak moment, Stephen Dallas, the mill owner's son, marries Stella Martin, a millworker's daughter. By the time their daughter, Laurel, is ten, Stephen is far away at his New York City job, and Stella is keeping time—not explicitly sexual, more for laughs—with the boisterous, borderline-repellent Ed Munn. The Munn connection further befouls the odor of Stella's reputation among the small-town gentry, and Laurel is denied access to a private school for young ladies of good background.

Now a teenager with an unblemished soul and impeccable demeanor, Laurel has fallen in love with Richard, a plutocrat, and he with her. When Stella overhears

Madame X, 1937: In the remake just eight years later, Gladys George
is the notorious defendant, John Beal her unknowing son.

mocking comments about her by Laurel's friends, who say that Richard would never marry a girl with "*that* mother," she leaps into expiatory action. She visits Helen Morrison, the refined widow whom Stephen has been courting in New York, saying she will agree to divorce him if Helen raises Laurel as her own. Yet the girl, still ferociously faithful to her mother, refuses to leave home. How can Stella push her daughter into the destiny she deserves in New York? By turning Laurel against her. By announcing she's about to marry Ed Munn. The trick works. Stephen and Helen marry, and then Laurel and Richard, in a wedding Stella doesn't feel worthy of joining. She stands outside, in a final gesture of sanctified masochism, to see that her little girl has found happiness in the upper class.

The challenge of the three *Stella Dallas* films, which spanned two-thirds of a century and ended with Bette Midler's endearing if anachronistic *Stella* in 1990, is to portray a woman who is crass in her behavior but harbors class in her heart. Gaudy and gauche, Stella is the sort of woman whose voice rises rudely above the murmurs on a train, as the more decorous riders flee to other cars. She is the "loathly lady" from Chaucer's Wife of Bath tale, and for viewers to sympathize with her, they must be shown how much she loves her daughter and how fully that love is reciprocated. (The plot might have been more piquant if Laurel, as she matured into a young lady, had been tempted to renounce her mother as a route to the social acceptance she craved—if she had said, "I'm ashamed of the mother I love." But that's another story: *Imitation of Life*.)

Screenwriter Frances Marion establishes the Stella-Laurel bond early in the 1925 **Stella Dallas**, directed by Henry King and starring Belle Bennett. Of the infant Laurel, Stella tells Stephen (Ronald Colman), "Maybe I haven't been much of a mother, but I love my baby—and I'd die if she were taken away from me." Whatever kind of mother she may be, she's quite a sight. Strutting through town in her mismatched faux finery, she stokes an almost Technicolor riot in the black and white film, and, though the movie is silent, when Stella is shown sleeping you can practically hear her snore. But Laurel (persuasively impersonated from the ages of ten to twenty by sixteen-year-old Lois Moran) can see the character behind this cartoon. And just as important as Laurel's love is Stella's snooty dismissal by "nice people." They shake her

Stella Dallas, 1925: Belle Bennett as the frowsy Stella, Ronald Colman as her husband,
Stephen, and Jean Hersholt as the ungentlemanly caller.

hand as if it were a decayed fish, boycott the birthday party she has thrown for Laurel and libel her within her hearing: "To think that that dreadful creature we saw today is Laurel's mother! . . . A mother like that is a millstone around her neck." Rather than exposing Stella's deficiencies, these rejections serve to solder Laurel's loyalty. Stella becomes her daughter's great lost cause.

For Stella to convince both Laurel and the audience of her noble renunciation, she needs a confederate: Helen (Alice Joyce), the woman her husband wants to marry, and the mother of three boys. "Why no," she protests to Stella, "I couldn't rob a mother of her only little girl." Stella presses her point: "I'd like people to think she's yours. You're the kind of a mother she could be proud of; I—I ain't. . . . She'll never be nobody with me shackled around one foot." The girl will be moving up and not lacking the love of a good woman. In fact, Helen has already prepared Laurel's bedroom, which is about the size of the old Penn Station concourse; on the bed pillow, Stella plants a moist kiss. An intertitle describes Stella and Helen as "two mothers, united by an understanding beyond words." Their benign conspiracy doesn't change Laurel's mind until Stella's letter announcing her alliance with Ed Munn (Jean Hersholt). Helen is not fooled, saying to Stephen, "That pitiful letter—couldn't you read between the lines?" Indulgent but myopic, he replies, "Helen dear, you see with the eyes of an angel." And, in a line that reveals a woman's empathy in reading another woman's soul, Helen says, "No, Stephen—*with the eyes of a mother*."

(Here the writer pauses to compose himself, wipe his own eyes and continue.)

Barbara Stanwyck was no dewy damsel. Like James Cagney, her male equivalent at Warners in the early thirties, she carried the flag of the urban poor, with all their hard-won wisdom, their skepticism, their knowing which rules to play by and which to disregard. Many of her films were fables of the underclass fighting the privileged class, and winning. So Stanwyck seemed an odd choice for the leading role in the 1937 *Stella Dallas*—where the war of the classes was the film's subject, not just its subtext, and where the screen's toughest cookie would impersonate a self-sacrificing back-street mother. How could a character played by brassy Barbara Stanwyck be willing to forfeit her husband (John Boles) and her daughter (Anne Shirley) to another woman (Barbara O'Neil, who two years later played Scarlett's mother, the

Stella Dallas, 1937: Barbara Stanwyck in the frock with the marshmallow
sleeves and Anne Shirley as her loving daughter, Laurel.

matriarch of Tara, in *Gone With the Wind*) and consign herself to the company of
that belligerent oaf Ed Munn (Alan Hale)?

In this King Vidor version, Stanwyck plays Stella hard and broad, almost taunting the audience to dismiss her. The former Broadway dancer strides across the room,
cranking her arms like a fast-walk marathoner. The sleek clotheshorse sports a dress
that resembles a giant banana split, with oversize marshmallows for triceps. She
often shouts her lines, as if trying to drown out the voices in Stella's head telling her
she's not good enough. At times, Stanwyck seems outside her character, commenting
on and subverting the sentiment that the 1925 film embraced; she will cue the audience to pity Stella here, despise her there. But that is her genius. She pushes viewers'
sympathy away, then draws it in like a master angler. At the end, resplendent in the

serious actress's "no-makeup" makeup look, Stanwyck has transformed skeptics—the ones she created in the first half of the film—into true believers. For once, this classy underclass dame told an audience that the poor should leave their best dream, their children, in the care of the upper class. And nothing in Stanwyck's moist eyes and triumphant smile, at the final fadeout, says that she doesn't believe it herself.

ANNA KARENINA

"All happy families are alike," begins Leo Tolstoy's 1875–77 novel. "Each unhappy family is unhappy in its own way." Brought to the big or small screen a couple dozen times, in Germany, Italy, Argentina, and of course Russia, *Anna Karenina* offered the domestic tragedy of a dutiful wife betraying her stuffy husband and precious son for the unreliable affection of Count Vronsky, in a liaison that leads to ostracism and death. The character gave meaty roles to Greta Garbo—twice, in the silent *Love* and a talkie remake—and to Vivien Leigh and Keira Knightley. The last might seem a distant third in competition with a pair of cinema's most incandescent actresses, but Knightley gives the boldest interpretation of the woman who, as generations of schoolchildren and moviegoers know, threw herself under a train after her adulterous passion turned to ashes.

Love (1927), directed in lambent, late-silent-film fashion by Edmund Goulding, cast Garbo opposite the Vronsky of John Gilbert, MGM's silent dreamboat and, at the time, the actress's off-screen paramour. "John Gilbert and Greta Garbo in *Love*," the posters proclaimed, as if the movie were a gossip headline. The studio might also have been acknowledging that this wasn't exactly Tolstoy's story, since screenwriter Frances Marion contrived to give Anna a happy ending. (Three years after they part, Karenin dies and the lovers are reunited.) Of all the Vronskys, Gilbert's is the rare one to court Anna without realizing that she is married; he is also the most smitten by, and loyal to, the woman on whom he would brand a social stigma. And Garbo was playing the femme fatale established in her earlier movies. To her lovers she was an obsession; to her husbands, only an ornament. Karenin (Brandon Hurst), with dead eyes and a sewn-on scowl, cares not about her

Love, 1927: Garbo as Anna Karenina with Philippe De Lacy as her seraphic son.

faithlessness but about his position. "I may find it convenient not to know," he says in the intertitles. "I shall do nothing [until] you have made public your guilt." That happens soon enough, followed by Karenin's painful penalty: forbidding Anna to see their son, Serezha.

In any Garbo film, the camera is her true mirror and lover. But both of her *Anna Karenina*s place her son, not Vronsky, near the center of Anna's heart. Played in *Love* by the seraphic nine-year-old Philippe De Lacy, Serezha exudes a pre-Raphaelite sensuality that makes him the ideal love object for a repressed and doting mother. When Anna and Serezha meet after a long separation, he takes her head in his hands as he kisses it from above, in patented Garbo style. She gives him many loving pats on all four cheeks. Not that the relationship is creepily incestuous—only that Anna is more suited to being a mother than a mistress, and that Serezha, as her son, will be ever faithful to the woman who bore him. Because, after all, she's Garbo.

The difference between Freddie Bartholomew, who played Garbo's son (here called Sergei) in the 1935 *Anna Karenina*, and De Lacy is the difference between an asexual fawn and an androgynous satyr, between Peter Pan and pagan Pan. Anyway, Bartholomew needn't have radiated preadolescent warmth in competition with Vronsky, since Fredric March is starchy and sexless in the role. (Perhaps Garbo was in part to blame for that. Director Clarence Brown later recalled that, when March "showed signs of wanting to get romantic . . . before each love scene Garbo put a small piece of garlic in her mouth.") The more powerful character is Basil Rathbone's Karenin, a figure of preening righteousness who is jealous less of her passion for her lover than of her devotion to her son—a bond that excludes him. When Karenin surprises Anna during her clandestine visit to Sergei, he orders her out of the house. As Garbo walks down the grand staircase and out the door, her posture becomes more stooped, with all the albatrosses of a disapproving Russian society on her lustrous shoulders. She knows she will never see her son again. A rendezvous with the train awaits.

Between her signature Hollywood roles as Scarlett O'Hara in *Gone With the Wind* and Blanche DuBois in *A Streetcar Named Desire*, Leigh played Emma Hamilton to her husband Laurence Olivier's Lord Nelson in *Lady Hamilton* (*That Hamilton Woman* in the United States), Cleopatra to Claude Rains's Julius Caesar and, in 1948, *Anna Karenina*. Director Julien Duvivier surrounded Leigh with one towering presence—Ralph Richardson as Karenin—and two actors who made little impression in their important roles: twenty-three-year-old Kieron Moore as Vronsky and Patrick Skipwith (in his only film appearance) as Sergei. Both are, in effect, her doomed boys—the charges to whom she imparts her tragic wisdom—even as Karenin treats her less as a wife than as a misbehaving daughter. From the first scene, in a train to Moscow, where Anna shows a picture of her adored son to a stranger who we soon learn is Vronsky's mother, to her final farewell to Sergei, Leigh summons a fiery maternal love. But the movie produces more visual smoke than emotional steam in chugging toward its tragic destination.

Joe Wright's brazen, exhilarating *Anna Karenina* (2012), scripted by Tom Stoppard, reimagines the Tolstoy story as comic opera that blooms into grand opera. Wright stages most of the action in a reproduction of a nineteenth-century theater, while Sidi Larbi Cherkaoui's virtuoso choreography sets dozens of characters awhirl

Anna Karenina, 1935: Basil Rathbone as Karenin, Greta Garbo as Anna and Freddie Bartholomew as their son prove that this unhappy family is different.

and aghast at the reckless affair that Anna (Keira Knightley), wife of a respected judge (Jude Law), pursues with the dashing Vronsky (Aaron Taylor-Johnson). All the world, the world of the Russian aristocracy, becomes the stage on which the lovers play out their scandalous affair.

Knightley's Anna is the girlish wife of a good, gray man for whom she feels respect; her love is poured into their beautiful son, Serhoza (Oskar McNamara). Once smitten with the precocious Vronsky, who might be Serhoza a dozen years older, she is raised to heavenly ecstasy before tumbling into the abyss of shame. It's a nervy performance, acutely attuned to the volcanic changes that a naïve creature must enjoy and endure on her first leap into mad passion. Wright allows more sympathy for Law's Karenin, a decent fellow stunned by his wife's betrayal, than for Taylor-Johnson's Vronsky, a primping soldier somewhat startled to realize that his lovely conquest thinks the tryst is eternal love. Why would Anna risk not just her marriage but access to her son? It's just not sensible. But that is Wright's—perhaps Tolstoy's—point: that motherhood is a mature commitment and adulterous passion a meteorological accident.

IMITATION OF LIFE

"Hope for the best, expect the worst. / You could be Tolstoy or Fannie Hurst." Mel Brooks's lyric for a song from his 1970 film *The Twelve Chairs* expressed the received opinion of the novelists' relative literary merits. Hollywood had a different opinion. From Tolstoy's novels it made expensive adaptations only of *Anna Karenina* and *Resurrection*, filmed as 1934's *We Live Again*, with Fredric March this time seducing Anna Sten. (The 1956 *War and Peace* was Italian producer Dino De Laurentiis's big idea.)

Hurst, though, was movie gold. *Back Street*, detailing the decades-long affair of a working-class woman and the banker who loves her but will never leave his wife and kids, got spun into three Universal weepies: with Irene Dunne in 1932, Margaret Sullavan in 1941 and Susan Hayward in 1961. Hurst's novel *Sister Act*, about a widowed father and his musical family, birthed Warner Bros.' *Four Daughters* (with Claude Rains, Gale Page and the three Lane sisters) in 1938, plus two sequels and the 1954 musical remake *Young at Heart*. A Hurst short story became Warners' *Humoresque*

(1946), in which a mother (Ruth Nelson) encourages her son (John Garfield) to pursue his career as a violinist and warns him against entanglement with his benefactress (Joan Crawford). But all these were the merest lace valentines compared with the films made from Hurst's 1933 novel *Imitation of Life*: director John M. Stahl's in 1934 and Douglas Sirk's in 1959. These two hit the jackpot, both as mother-daughter tales and as potent parables for an America mired in racial confusion.

The star billing for the two movies—Claudette Colbert, Warren William and Rochelle Hudson in 1934, Lana Turner, John Gavin and Sandra Dee in 1959—suggests that the story is about a widowed woman whose stalwart beau becomes the object of her daughter's affections. Mother and child fighting over the same man? Can't-miss melodrama. Actually, that is only the docile subplot in a much more volatile generational tangle: between the leading lady's African-American maid and her daughter, who is so light-skinned she can pass for white. She does so, breaking both the color barrier and her mother's heart.

The 1959 **Imitation of Life**, described by Dave Kehr in *The New York Times* as "a Lana Turner soap opera turned into an exercise in metaphysical formalism by Sirk's finely textured and densely layered images," earned Oscar nominations for both Juanita Moore (as Annie, the mother) and Susan Kohner (as Sarah Jane, the daughter). The climactic scene of Annie's funeral, when Sarah Jane throws herself on her mother's coffin to beg forgiveness, sticks in the viewer's gut as one of the signature movie moments of repentance and catharsis.

Kohner was born of mixed ethnic legacy. Her father was the Czech-Jewish Paul Kohner, the renowned agent who had worked as a producer at Universal on late silent and early sound films, including the 1931 Spanish-language version of *Dracula*. Her mother was Lupita Tovar, the Mexican actress who played the female lead in *Dracula*'s Spanish-language "remake," which was shot at night on the same sets used for the Bela Lugosi picture. (Susan's sons became directors: Paul with *American Pie*, Chris with *About a Boy*.) Kohner pours a nervy sensuousness into Sarah Jane; she radiates light in her attempts to enter posh society by seeming Caucasian, and heat in her verbal takedown of the clearly outmatched Lana. Annie sympathizes with Sarah Jane's dilemma, asking, "How do you tell a child that she was born to be hurt?" But

Imitation of Life, 1959: Lana Turner and her daughter Susie (Terry Burnham) with Juanita Hall and her light-skinned Sarah Jane (Karin Dicker); the grown-up girls would later be played by Sandra Dee and Susan Kohner.

the young woman crushes her mother's spirit by refusing to attend "a colored teachers' college," by denying the legacy of her mother and her race, and by proclaiming, "I'm somebody else. I'm white . . . white . . . *white!*"

The social and racial vectors of the 1934 ***Imitation of Life*** are even more wrenching, both on-screen and in the two actresses' biographies. The black mother, Delilah (Louise Beavers), has devised a pancake recipe that makes a fortune for her employer Bea (Colbert). Delilah is now a millionaire, sharing a mansion with Bea. The two women share an affection and respect unusual for films of that period; they are partners in business and in the mutual raising of their two kids. Yet Delilah's wealth never gives her a feeling of equality with whites. She insists on sleeping in the basement, as she always did, with her rebellious daughter Peola (Fredi Washington).

Peola's wonderful mother is exactly the wrong mother for her, so far apart are their respective ideas of what is possible and proper. When the girl leaves home and finds a job as a restaurant cashier, Delilah begs her to come home, and Peola denies her mom, as Peter did Jesus. "Even if you pass me on the street," she later says, "you'll have to pass me by." Bea is shocked by this callousness, but Peola tells her, "You don't know what it's like to look white and be black. You don't know. I can't go on this way any longer!" Washington's plangent contralto makes this line a heartbreaker.

The stocky, Christmas-angel-faced Beavers, who had worked as a maid to silent screen star Leatrice Joy (Mrs. John Gilbert), went on to play maids in many movies; she also followed Ethel Waters and Hattie McDaniel as the problem-solving maid in the early-fifties sitcom *Beulah*. But the true revelation and pathos come from Washington, an elegant, light-skinned beauty born of black parents in 1903. Getting work in Dudley Murphy's indie films of the early sound era, she played Duke Ellington's dancer girlfriend in 1929's *Black and Tan* and a prostitute opposite Paul Robeson in 1933's *The Emperor Jones* (where makeup darkened her skin so viewers would not think Robeson was consorting with a white woman). Washington's exotic outsider status pursued her, defined her, wherever she went. She occasionally accompanied her husband, trombonist Lawrence Brown, with the Duke Ellington orchestra on dates in the American South. Josephine Baker's adopted son Jean-Claude has said that the black musicians "could not go into ice cream parlors, so she would go in and buy the

ice cream, then go outside and give it to Ellington and the band. Whites screamed at her, 'N—— lover!'" To feed her friends, Washington really did pass for white.

In those days the word "passing" had an almost tragic heft. It meant not only secretly renouncing one's race but becoming a "real" American—to enjoy the privileges of equality and anonymity, at a time when a tenth of all citizens were denied access to voting booths, hotels, restaurants, restrooms and a fair shake from the white majority. "America" was a club whose membership numbered 120 million or so, all of them white. Why shouldn't someone who looked as if she belonged in the club try to join it, if only as a kind of double agent? So Peola decides that, to escape second-class citizenry and be accepted by whites, she must convince them that she is "one of them." Gliding on the edges of white society, she wonders why, if her mother's employer could ascend to its elevated center through money, a light-skinned young woman couldn't get there with prettiness.

At least, in the two versions of *Imitation of Life*, Hollywood addressed the subject of passing—a clear metaphor for color-blindness. "I know it's asking a lot," Peola says. "But I've got to live my own life." On the movie's terms, this is only an imitation of life, a sham citizenship. Peola is a tragic figure whose quest is seen as a betrayal of mother, roots, self. And Washington, who lived to be ninety, got only one more role in a Hollywood film: *One Mile from Heaven* (1937), where she plays a "black" woman who claims that the "white" girl she cares for is her natural daughter.

IMITATION OF *IMITATION OF LIFE*

Like the United States, Mexico had a race problem. With much intermarrying between the indigenous population and the descendants of Spanish émigrés, the country was its own rainbow coalition, or contradiction. Most of the movie stars were light-skinned; those who weren't often played comic or villainous relief. And at least once, in its own golden age, the Mexico film industry didn't ignore the race

facing page: Imitation of Life, 1934: Louise Beavers and Sebie Hendricks (later Fredi Washington), with Claudette Colbert and Baby Jane Quigley (later Rochelle Hudson).

issue. Director Joselito Rodríguez's 1948 film **Little Black Angels** (*Angelitos Negros*) is officially based on a play by the Cuban Félix B. Caignet, but it's a transparent gloss on *Imitation of Life*: the story of a light-skinned woman who disdains all people of color—including her dark-skinned mother—without realizing that she is a member of the race she hates. Available with English subtitles in the Pedro Infante Collection from Warner Home Video, the movie is crucial, touching and bizarre.

Infante, the actor-singer megastar who was the Crosby, Sinatra and Elvis of 1940s–'50s Mexico, plays the nightclub entertainer José Carlos, deeply in love with Ana Luisa (Emilia Guiú), a blond schoolteacher who's snooty to those of darker hue. She's downright rude to José Carlos's Afro-Cuban bandmate, Fernando (Chimi Monterrey) and thinks that José Carlos's performing in blackface is demeaning, but he shrugs that off with a laugh: "You're very lucky: You're being courted by two men. A white one by day and a black one by night." As boy and girl get closer to marriage, unexpected opposition emerges from Ana Luisa's black maid Mercé (Rita Montaner), who has raised her selflessly since infancy; Ana Luisa believes she is an orphan. Mercé's reason for fighting the betrothal: she is Ana Luisa's mother, though she has never told the girl. Love has made Mercé endure both her maid status and the contempt her daughter sometimes shows her—as when she denies Mercé's plea to attend the wedding.

A year later, a child, Belén, is born, and her skin is dark. Ana Luisa, horrified, and fearful of being ostracized by her rich friends, blames José Carlos for having had black ancestors. Now would be the time to tell Ana Luisa where she came from, but the doctor says her heart is too weak to take a severe shock. Four years later, Belén (Titina Romay) is a darling child with the loving disposition of her father—and her grandmother. But Ana Luisa still resents and recoils from her: "Why didn't God send me a white, blond girl? I would have loved her so much." Desperate for affection from her mother, Belén puts pancake makeup on her face, saying, "I want to be white so Mama will love me." Touched by this poignant travesty, Ana Luisa kisses Belén for the first time.

Now the tensions boil over and the ironic dialogue gets hotter. Ana Luisa exclaims, in agony, "Oh, if only my mother were alive!" and, in anger, "I'd kill myself if

Little Black Angels, 1948: Pedro Infante cradles his dark-skinned daughter, flanked by the local priest (Nicholas Rodríguez) and the child's grandmother (Rita Montaner).

my mother were black." (Hearing that, José Carlos slaps her.) Mercé, ground down by the ill feelings, is getting weaker. And when Ana Luisa calls her a "damn black woman" and strikes her, José Carlos shouts the words that were denied to Ruth Chatterton and Gladys George in their *Madame X* films, but which this movie has been galloping toward: "Don't! She is your mother!" Shock; guilt; death; sensation! Cue tears that would flood the Rio Grande.

Pretty amazing, eh? The movie extends the subterfuge of *Imitation of Life*'s Peola, who knew her mother was black but needed to pass for white, to Ana Luisa, so at ease in her dismissal of blacks because she believes she *is* white. Finally learning the true color of her mother and herself, Ana Luisa must now accept all those of color or despise herself forever. But as unusual as the *Little Black Angels* narrative is, the casting is even stranger. Except for Monterrey, all the actors playing African or mixed-race characters, including Mercé and Belén, were white. The movie is a tale of mother love submerged in race hatred—a plea for harmony among people of all colors—done in blackface.

On Movie Motherhood

There are movie mothers, moms, mamas, maws and mums. Most of them were sweet, loving and caring, and taught us lessons to live by. But there were bad ones, too—like Mildred Pierce, played by Joan Crawford—who could put us on the wrong track.

There were many actresses who made wonderful movie moms: Barbara Stanwyck, Marlene Dietrich, Selena Royle, Ann Harding and more. To me, Fay Bainter was the perfect mom. She was gentle but strong and understanding—a complete mom. I don't know if she had any children or not, but she obviously liked children, or was a fantastic actress.

I played a mother once in *Seven Brides for Seven Brothers*, though that wasn't the focus of the film. It was a Technicolor musical, and like most musicals and most color films, it was not a "mother movie" per se (the black and white films focused strongly on character, whereas color seems to dissipate the drama). In a musical, mothering is rarely that important. You know it will be a short scene with lots and lots of music. But I had a couple of children of my own when I did this film, and because I wanted the children and adored the children, I didn't have to work at being a mother for this role.

Above all, I really miss the tearjerkers, but they are not in vogue today. I'll always remember my favorite, Irene Dunne in *I Remember Mama*. Irene had a great sense of whatever was needed, and an intelligent sense of humor that was catching and on the mark. I have always loved everything she did.

—*Jane Powell*

Gigi, 1958: Isabel Jeans instructs her niece Gigi (Leslie Caron) in the art of being a courtesan.

AUNTS

Sometimes another relative can step into the role.

Movie aunts come in two basic packages. One is the woman who may not be suited for motherhood but is obliged to assume the rearing of her absent sister's or brother's child. She tends to be the disciplinarian, almost a prison matron, imposing structure and strictures on a young, intrusive presence. If she has a child of her own, as Aunt Petunia Dursley does in the Harry Potter movies, she spoils her offspring and torments the foundling. The second type is the free spirit, a believer in inspiration over obedience. When a child is entrusted to her care, she teaches her most important, joyous lesson: to embrace life with a capital L.

In *Auntie Mame* (1958), Manhattan diva Mame Dennis (Rosalind Russell) offers her ten-year-old nephew Patrick (Jan Handzlik) a most liberal education, including enrollment in a Greenwich Village progressive school, where the children "romp around naked" playing Fish Families, and all the finest adult literature. When Patrick shows Mame a list of words he doesn't understand—"neurotic, heterosexual"—she says, "You won't need some of these words for months and months." As Patrick (now played by Roger Smith) grows stolid in young manhood in his twenties and gets engaged to a snooty "Aryan from Darien," Mame expertly scotches the alliance with one of her scandalous

Auntie Mame, 1958: Mame (Rosalind Russell) defends her nephew Patrick (Jan Handzlik) against the boy's stuffy lawyer (Fred Clark).

cocktail parties; as she serves flaming cocktails, she asks, "There now, are we all lit?" Plenty of men we know wish they'd been raised by Mame, who famously said, "Life's a banquet, and most poor suckers are starving to death!"

Patrick Dennis's education was downright Amish compared with the lessons that Leslie Caron in *Gigi* (1958) receives from her aunt Alicia (Isabel Jeans): how to be a courtesan. In Alan Jay Lerner and Frederick Loewe's original movie musical, based on a Colette novella and directed by Vincente Minnelli, teenage Gigi learns how to please a man, win his patronage and, when the game becomes tiresome, end it. "Marriage is not forbidden to us," Alicia tells the girl, "but instead of getting married at once, it sometimes happens we get married at last." Alicia's ethos is purely monetary: "Wait for the first-class jewels, Gigi. Hold on to your ideals." But this marvelous movie is a romance. When Gigi grows up and conquers the aristocrat Gaston (Louis Jourdan), they both shock their jaded relatives by falling into that bourgeois trap called love. Alicia has taught her student the price of everything; Gigi, on her own, learns the value of values.

More often, aunts are the stuffy beneficiaries of a child's fresh perspective. In Disney's 1960 version of *Pollyanna*, the Eleanor Porter novel that Mary Pickford had filmed forty years before, Hayley Mills is the orphan who revives the spirit of rich, crabby Aunt Polly (Jane Wyman). While Polly teaches the girl good posture, Pollyanna helps her aunt relax, enjoy life and let the town build a new orphanage. Even a brief case of paralyzed legs can't wipe the smile permanently from this Miss Sunshine, who manages to implant a smile in Aunt Polly's Grinchy heart.

Any adaptation of Mark Twain's *Tom Sawyer*, like David O. Selznick's 1938 film, will put his guardian at a disadvantage. May Robson's Aunt Polly must be the disciplinarian whose strategies backfire—as when she punishes Tom (Tommy Kelly) for his playing hooky by insisting he whitewash the fence and he persuades other boys to do the job—and who, for all her sensible strictures, can never wrest sympathy from the spirit of impish, impious youth that Twain created. Robson clucks at Tom and all but winks at the audience, to show her, if not Polly's, complicity in the fun.

Robson was at one time set for the role of Auntie Em in *The Wizard of Oz* (1939). The part went instead to Clara Blandick, who had played Aunt Polly in the

1938 Twain sequel *Tom Sawyer, Detective.* Her casting would make Em perhaps the most perplexing figure in the canon of movie aunts. She is a woman worn from running the Gale farm; her husband Henry (Charley Grapewin) and the three farmhands (Ray Bolger, Jack Haley and Bert Lahr), who will later show up in Oz, are clearly her subordinates. When her niece Dorothy (Judy Garland) begs for attention—evil Miss Gulch (Margaret Hamilton) wants to dognap Toto—Em, preoccupied with the urgency of counting chickens, dismisses her with a "Find yourself a place where you won't get into any trouble." That would be a corner of the farm where Dorothy sings "Over the Rainbow." With the aid of a cyclone and a bump on the head, Dorothy is in Oz. Black and white becomes ravishing Technicolor, and a solitary girl defeats the Wicked Witch and saves the kingdom. She has escaped prosaic Kansas for the poetry of Oz, the mundane dialogue of the farm for the immortal songs of the Emerald City. In the scarecrow, the Tin Man and the Cowardly Lion, Dorothy has found the family she dreamed of.

Frank Morgan's Professor Marvel, later the Wizard, must teach the runaway Dorothy—and the audience—that Em's stern ways conceal a love for her niece. He says that her aunt is near death from worry, because "Someone has just about broken her heart . . . someone she loves very much." The movie hasn't exactly shown us this; the Em on screen looks like a Dust Bowl refugee in a Dorothea Lange photo and behaves like Ma Joad without the fiery optimism. She may well be a woman, like the mother in *A Tree Grows in Brooklyn*, who feels love for the girl but hasn't the gift of expressing it—of taking time from her duties to caress and console a lonely niece. But when the Professor intuits (really, invents) Em's tender feelings, Dorothy believes it.

That is why, throughout her stay in the Merry Old Land of Oz, the orphan girl keeps yearning to return to Kansas and Auntie Em. She decides that the mother figure she has thought of as an oppressor is really her guardian angel—that the rainbow is in Auntie Em's heart. Dorothy has convinced herself that, whatever the seductions of Oz, she can find happiness back in her own farmyard.

The Wizard of Oz, 1939: Dorothy (Judy Garland) petitions her Auntie Em (Clara Blandick) and Uncle Henry (Charley Grapewin) to save Toto from the clutches of the wicked old Miss Gulch (Margaret Hamilton).

Gone With the Wind, 1939: Who pulls the strings at Tara— Scarlett (Vivien Leigh) or Mammy (Hattie McDaniel)?

MAMMIES AND NANNIES

They pour their love or pain into other people's children.

The very word "mammy" is antique, anachronistic and possibly offensive. It summons a vision of the Old South that is, to modern sensibilities, a magnolia-scented gulag where black slaves toiled in the fields to sustain a cotton economy or worked in the owners' houses as a permanent indentured servant class. Director Steve McQueen's *12 Years a Slave*, based on the memoir of a free Northern black man sold into Southern bondage, serves as scalding testimony to a stained era.

Yet in those houses, and in the less ornate homes of the South for a century after the Confederacy collapsed, women of color could speak the truth of the powerless to whites, share the affectionate kinship of sisterhood with the women in charge and infuse their values in the de facto raising of white children. If Mammy in *Gone With the Wind* has no name but her job, she still is a brave and formidable woman—an elemental force recognized by the Academy of Motion Picture Arts and Sciences when, in 1940, it made Hattie McDaniel the first African-American to win an Oscar for Best Supporting Actress.

Gone With the Wind (1939), which in terms of tickets sold is still the most popular movie of all time, is remembered as the love story of Scarlett O'Hara (Vivien Leigh) and Rhett Butler (Clark Gable). Misremembered, really, since the object of Scarlett's true and unrequited ardor is the prim aristocrat Ashley Wilkes (Leslie Howard). She marries Rhett not for his sex appeal, which was evident to every female in the movie audience, but for his money, which will restore her social standing after the Civil War and maintain her estate. Indeed, Scarlett's abiding beau—her constant lover and the spur to her ambition—is the land, Tara. Producer David O. Selznick's film, no less than the Margaret Mitchell novel that spawned it, is really about real estate, the eternal obsession of field marshals and homemakers alike. Less a war movie than a woman's picture, *GWTW* stints on the men's battlefield exploits and sticks with the home-front females: Scarlett, Ashley's demure bride Melanie (Olivia de Havilland) and the Tara house servants Mammy (Hattie McDaniel) and Prissy (Butterfly McQueen).

Scarlett, for all her Southern-belle airs, is a modern businesswoman, as ingenious and ruthless as any man in rebuilding her wealth. Trained to dominate by charm, she is unschooled in all the skills Mammy possesses—including bossing Scarlett to uphold the honor of Tara. "If you don't care what folks says about dis family, I does!" she thunders, making sure her famished employer eats some food. It is Mammy who summons Melanie to Tara after the death of Scarlett's and Rhett's daughter, Bonnie. She stares smoldering disapproval at Rhett, chides Scarlett for continuing to moon after Ashley and carries much of the narrative in her capacious bosom. Scarlett may be Tara's mistress, but Mammy is its muscle and heart.

The Member of the Wedding, 1952: Ethel Waters comforts Julie Harris and Brandon deWilde.

The black servant class persisted long after the official end of segregation; en masse, it has raised several hundred years of white children. In ***The Member of the Wedding*** (1952), from Carson McCullers's novel and play, the housekeeper Berenice Sadie Brown (Ethel Waters) takes care of Frankie Addams, a twelve-year-old tomboy (played by twenty-seven-year-old Julie Harris). In a Southern backwater in late summer, the impossible dreams are the most fervent: Frankie wants to accompany her older brother and his bride to Alaska. With her mother dead and her father absent, Frankie begrudges Berenice's attempts to impose discipline but accepts her moral authority. A black woman is the only friend, the only mother figure, this white girl has.

Another Southern story: In New Orleans in 1918, a child is born who looks like a tiny old man—a wrinkled thing with cataracts, arthritis and a murderer's curse on his head; his mother died giving birth to him. Thus begins ***The Curious Case of Benjamin Button*** (2008), the expansion by screenwriter Eric Roth and director

David Fincher of F. Scott Fitzgerald's 1922 fable about a person who was born an old man and got younger each day for the rest of his long life. His father leaves Benjamin (Brad Pitt) on the steps of an old folks' home, where he is cared for by a black maid, Queenie (Taraji P. Henson), who cradles him with a mother's love, saying, "You as ugly as an old pot, but you still a child of God." In this nursery for the aged, death is the biggest part of life; that suits Benjamin, who was born with an old man's wisdom—the knowledge that every story has a beginning and an end, even if they run in opposite directions. Benjamin never forgets Queenie through his *Forrest Gump*-ish series of adventures, though of course he outlives her. Courting the

The Help, 2011: Cicely Tyson, the matriarch of maids, with the young Skeeter (Lila Rogers).

beautiful Daisy (Cate Blanchett), he becomes her husband and, as he spirals into his teens, tweens and infancy, her most beloved child.

Finally, Jackson, Mississippi, in the 1960s, a full century after the Civil War. White women live in fancy homes, not plantation mansions, but they still have women darker than themselves to cook the food and mind the babies. An ensemble morality play, *The Help* (2011), directed by Tate Taylor from Kathryn Stockett's novel, draws its characters in broad, swift strokes, so that the heroines and harridans are instantly distinguishable. Black is beautiful and white is either hateful or naïve— unless the white person is the Stockett stand-in Skeeter (Emma Stone), herself raised by a woman of color (Cicely Tyson) and now planning a book of testimony by the town's black maids. In itemizing the small-mindedness of the ruling class, the film raises admiration for the maids and outrage at the contempt with which their employers treat them. There is ferocious moral power in the saintly stoicism of Viola Davis's Aibileen and a stoic warmth in Octavia Spencer's Minny, for whom revenge is a dish best served as a chocolate pie. Davis was nominated for a Best Actress Oscar, and Spencer won for Supporting Actress. Hattie McDaniel would be pleased.

Blossoms in the Dust, 1941: Foundling-home founder Greer Garson and her brood of "illegitimate" children.

A MOM BY
ANY OTHER NAME

Because it's the right thing to do.

The misanthropic wit Oscar Levant told this brief fable: "A son murders his mother and cuts her heart out to present to his sweetheart. . . . In his hurry he stumbles, and the disembodied heart that he clutches in his hand cries out, 'Did you hurt yourself, son?'" Levant's explanation, that "the mother's solicitude for her son was unimpaired," assumes a bond that extends from womb to tomb—and, in this case, beyond it. But the maternal spirit can also fill a woman who didn't give birth to the objects of her love. Sometimes

107

she inherits a child from the wife of a previous marriage. Sometimes kids just show up, and instinct or ethics or bravado compels a woman to let them stay. She may find a lonely child on a foundling-home doorstep, on the mean streets or on a deserted hilltop mansion. Whatever the circumstances, these women become mothers because it is the right thing to do. Their Bible lesson might be: Suffer the little children, that they suffer no more.

MOTHERS OF LOST CHILDREN

A woman's kindness toward children can be indiscriminate; she opens her arms to all wounded creatures. Edna Kahly Gladney (Greer Garson) in **Blossoms in the Dust** (1941) founded the Texas Children's Home and Aid Society of Fort Worth, which gave shelter, education and, crucially, legal legitimacy to children of unwed parents. Gladney, herself born out of wedlock, persuaded the Texas state senate to strike the word "illegitimate" from birth records, declaring in a gallery speech that galvanized listeners (and earned Garson her first of five consecutive Best Actress Oscar nominations) that "there are no illegitimate children. There are only illegitimate parents."

"It's a hard world for little things," says Rachel Cooper (Lillian Gish) in **The Night of the Hunter** (1955), the miracle of mood, depredation and redemption directed by Charles Laughton and scripted by James Agee from Davis Grubb's novel. In the West Virginia swamps of the 1930s, Rachel has no government approval, only a selfless impulse to collect unwanted children. John Harper (Billy Chapin) and his younger sister, Pearl (Sally Jane Bruce), need her intervention. Their father has been hanged, after first hiding his stolen money; their mother, Willa (Shelley Winters), has fallen for the Reverend Harry Powell (Robert Mitchum), who wants that money and will threaten the children or marry Willa—and worse—to get it. As seductively malevolent as Powell is, with his baritone parables and the words L-O-V-E and H-A-T-E tattooed on his knuckles, so beatifically empowered is Rachel, describing herself as "a strong tree with branches for many birds."

Edna and Rachel give homes to the young that society has discarded. Christine Collins, played by Angelina Jolie in Clint Eastwood's **Changeling** (2008), loses the

The Night of the Hunter, 1955: Lillian Gish protects Ruby (Gloria Castilo)
and her other foundling children with love and a rifle.

person she loves most: her nine-year-old boy Walter (Gattlin Griffith, later Kate Winslet's son in *Labor Day*). Several weeks after his disappearance, which triggers a highly publicized manhunt, word comes that the boy has been located. Instantly Christine sees that this "Walter" (Devon Conti) is not her son; but the police insist that he is. Case closed. When she points out the obvious differences in height and dental records, the officer in charge (Jeffrey Donovan) orders her confined to a psychiatric ward.

Based on the notorious Wineville Chicken Coop case, *Changeling* is an indictment of the corruption rampant in the municipal government, the police department and the medical establishment of Los Angeles in the 1920s; it's almost *Chinatown*, for real. As a heartbroken mother determined to find her son, dead or alive, Jolie fights on through a stream of tears; her sighs come with shrugs worthy of Atlas. Sleuthing at great personal risk and in a mire of depravity, Jolie's Christine is a real-life hero of the old, urban West, with no weapon but her inexhaustible love.

STEPMOTHERS

Moviegoers would have to wait until 1965 for a luminous portrait of a stepmother—first, granted, a nun postulant and a governess—who charmed seven children and their stern father by singing to them in the Austrian hills. A Best Picture Oscar winner and, in real dollars, still the third-biggest hit in American box-office history (after *Gone With the Wind* and *Star Wars*), Robert Wise's **The Sound of Music** (1965) built on Julie Andrews's skill with children as the nanny in the previous year's *Mary Poppins*. Her character, Maria, served as an antidote to all rotten stepmoms, an inspiration to children with a "new" mother and, in more recent years, camp fodder for the revival engagements of the *Sing-a-Long-a Sound of Music*, at which the audience dressed in convent or Tyrolean garb and warbled the Rodgers and Hammerstein secular hymns in harmony with Maria.

By that time the traditional family structure had been sundered into postnuclear shards; more than a third of all kids had stepmothers, and these second-class citizens of golden age movies saw Hollywood toss some affirmative-action love their way.

The Sound of Music, 1965: Julie Andrews, in her transformation from governess to stepmother of the von Trapp children.

(Though they might not always have loved the results.) Director Chris Columbus's *Stepmom* (1998), in which Isabel Kelly (Julia Roberts) marries the ex-husband of Jackie Harrison (Susan Sarandon) and must try to control her two new children, gaudily mixed the zingers of sassy sitcom kids with the emotional blackmail of Jackie's cancer. All this banter and badgering nearly obscures Jackie's sensible homily about two-mother families: "They don't have to choose. They can have us both. I have their past, you can have their future." But please: tens of millions stepmothering in domestic America, and this is how Hollywood addresses the issue?

Now we move on to another death, this time of a child, in a much better movie, Don Roos's *The Other Woman* (made in 2008, released in 2011), from Ayelet Waldman's novel *Love and Other Impossible Pursuits*. Emilia (Natalie Portman) had set her sights on Jack (Scott Cohen), her law firm's new boss, and pretty much seduced him away from his obstetrician wife Carolyn (Lisa Kudrow). Soon after they were married they had a daughter, Isabel, who died just after coming home from the maternity ward. A few years later, Emilia is still adjusting to losing Isabel while being a mother, kind of, to Jack and Carolyn's son, Will (Charlie Tahan).

As a second wife who in many eyes still wears a home-wrecker tag, Emilia has two missions: to win Will over from his efficient, stern mom, and to earn membership in the boys' club at home. Jack needs constant reassurance that he hasn't broken his first family for a failed second time around. Emilia must connect with Will because it might prove her marriage a success. Eventually they build an intimacy of equals, which for Will is a different sort of bond from the one he shares with his father, but warmer and just as strong. The relationship isn't at all romantic, but by the end she's become Will's first girl friend. If *The Other Woman* turns Wife No. 1 into a caricature and the husband into a cipher, it eventually ingratiates by the connection of young Tahan and Portman, in what is arguably her subtlest and most natural performance. Her Emilia is a woman wrestling with demons who overcomes them when she discovers that one of her opponents—her balky stepson—just showed up in her corner.

· · ·

The Other Woman, 2011: Natalie Portman tries making peace with her stepson, Charlie Tahan.

SURROGATE MOMS

In the decades when an unwed woman with a child could stoke scandal and banishment from polite society, Hollywood occasionally played the story as a comedy of mistaken identity. In ***Bachelor Mother*** (1939), Ginger Rogers is a salesgirl who notices an abandoned newborn on the steps of a foundling home on Christmas Eve and takes it inside to hand to the authorities. They think she's the mother, and so do the owner of her department store (Charles Coburn) and his playboy son (David Niven). She must declare the child her own, tapping her own unexpected yen for motherhood and winning, under the rules of romantic comedy, a rich husband and a richer father-in-law, who overcomes curmudgeonly scruples to declare, "I don't care who's the father—I'm the grandfather!" In similar style, two young masters of romantic comedy movies, screenwriter Norman Krasna and director Garson Kanin, evaded Production Code prudence and created this effervescent charmer of a movie about the unwed nonmother who became a wed mother.

Everything's proper in ***The King and I*** (1956), director Walter Lang's film of the

Bachelor Mother, 1939: David Niven suspects that the infant
Ginger Rogers is feeding is her own baby.

Rodgers and Hammerstein Broadway hit. The widow Anna Leonowens (Deborah Kerr) has come with her young son to Siam as governess to the children of the King (Yul Brynner) in the mid-nineteenth century. Anna and the King are each emotionally isolated: she as a widow and a foreigner, he as a monarch bred to believe in his own infallibility. When they finally, lightly touch in the majestic "Shall We Dance?" it has the thrilling impact of two worlds colliding in harmony. The King is weaned from his stubbornness by seeing Anna's deft connection with his kids. She teaches not just their schoolwork but also lessons in independence, even rebellion against their master. And he learns that a woman is more than a concubine; she is a professor of the civilizing impulse.

In its casting, the movie may rasp against modern ethnic sensitivity, let alone visual sense; none of the Siamese courtiers and only a few of the children are played by Asians. Yet this remains the most satisfying of all the story's film versions, which include Irene Dunne and Rex Harrison in *Anna and the King of Siam* in 1948, Jodie Foster and Chow Yun-fat in *Anna and the King* in 1999 and, the same year, an animated feature called *The King and I*. Brynner, in the role that defined his career, and Kerr, with her appealing blend of gentility and moral passion, make a lovely mismatched couple—stern father, warm mother—who tiptoe or polka to the brink of breaking convention. Shall they dance? Divinely. Will they consummate their affections? Impossible, im*poss*ible!

At the beginning of Tim Burton's **Edward Scissorhands** (1990), Peg the Avon lady (Dianne Wiest) wanders into a forbidding castle on a hill and discovers Edward (Johnny Depp), a grim automaton with shears at the ends of his arms. With equal parts salesmanship and motherly determination, she starts chattering: "Do you live up here all by yourself? What happened to your face? No, I won't hurt you. But at the

Edward Scissorhands, 1990: Dianne Wiest invites the boy with
the cutlery cuticles (Johnny Depp) to come live at her place.

The Blind Side, 2009: Sandra Bullock reads to her son (Jae Head) and her adopted son (Quinton Aaron).

very least, let me give you a good astringent." In a trice she has told the creature, "I think you should just come home with me." There, amid a quiet riot of coordinated pastels, she shows Edward pictures of her husband and kids, offers him the run of the refrigerator and gets him new clothes. Edward is the innocent other, a literary type that stretches from Kaspar Hauser to *Being There*'s Chauncey Gardiner, and Peg is the gentle mom of fifties sitcoms, approached for once with love, not derision. Despite her best efforts, this story of the Frankenstein monster as dreamboat will not end well, but it will end beautifully. Burton's career-long theme—of the misfit as gentle genius—gets its most bittersweet rendition here, perhaps because this time, the creature has a loving surrogate mom.

The Blind Side (2009) earned Sandra Bullock a Best Actress Oscar as Leigh Anne Tuohy, the Memphis mom who took in the homeless black teen Michael Oher (Quinton Aaron), prodding and coaching him toward football renown. In writer-director John Lee Hancock's film of the Michael Lewis nonfiction book, Leigh Anne struts through life with a scary assurance; she's a blond tornado, looking for people to challenge, causes to champion. Finding Michael gives her a goal that unites home, school and her preternatural ambition. It's as if Erin Brockovich had been given charge of E.T. What Leigh Anne sees in Michael is a gentle stillness; he's like a Buddha statue transplanted to Tennessee, and his only impediment to gridiron stardom is that he doesn't like to hurt people. Leigh Anne can solve that problem too. She has just the energy to push this soft boulder up the hill of achievement. No Miss Daisy was ever so driving.

The Blind Side has its cheesy moments, and its fable of a black child saved from his addict mother by a noble white woman allows for indelicate racial generalizations. But it offers a heroine rarely seen in modern movies (including Bullock movies). Too often, women with career drive are portrayed as rudderless and incomplete; they must end up being educated and tamed by men. But Bullock's Leigh Anne is a take-charge gal who pursues her vision and achieves it with very little help from men—and with no apologies. She has the holy mission, the elbows-out attitude and, let's say, the balls of a tough male film hero. Bullock could have dedicated her Oscar to all strong women, on-screen or off.

A Raisin in the Sun, 1961: A Chicago mother (Claudia McNeil) is torn between helping her two grown children (Sidney Poitier and Diana Sands) and realizing her own dream of a move to the suburbs.

WHEN MOMS COLLIDE WITH THEIR KIDS

Sometimes it's tough sharing space with a grown child.

On the "Babysitting" episode of NPR's *This American Life*, first broadcast in 2001, Myron Jones and his sister Carol Jones Bove, then near seventy, described being raised in 1940s Buffalo, New York, by their strict widowed mother—a woman so deficient in giving love or accepting it that her teenage kids invented a family for whom they said they babysat, just to get free of Mom for a few hours a night. Carol recalled, "When I was thirty-five, I lashed out at her . . . told her how I felt about her.

And she sat in a chair in the kitchen and she was crying. And I had never even seen her cry before. And when I finally stopped talking, she said, 'I did the very best I could.' And I thought, Oh my God, she did. Her best was so bad. Her best was so empty."

In the centuries before women's financial liberation, most men, even those of limited means, had some choice in their line of work: bootblack or bank teller, street sweeper or salesman. Women had many jobs—cook, housekeeper, child producer, teacher, nurse—under a single compound title: wife-mother. And aside from enduring this 24/7 grind, they were expected to seem to be enjoying it, as if the ordeal were a blessing, as if they were to whistle, and smile and nurture, while they worked. The law of averages would indicate that not all women were physically or emotionally suited to these demanding chores. Even if they did the very best they could, their children might judge the effort as bad or empty. Were the mothers at fault? The children? Or was it all a question of perspective? Maybe they just weren't suitable companions; husbands and wives sometimes take decades to come to that conclusion.

Here are a few examples of mothers and children whom personalities or circumstances put at emotional odds. Whether the figures are heroic or pathetic or comic, or a mixture of all three, they have trouble sharing the same space, especially when grown children live with their mothers. These psychodramas and psychological comedies recognize the truth of Amy Tan's observation, in *The Kitchen God's Wife*, "Whenever I'm with my mother, I feel as though I have to spend the whole time avoiding land mines."

"Seems like God didn't see fit to give the black man nothin' but dreams," says Lena Younger (Claudia McNeil), quoting her late husband, Big Walter, in *A Raisin in the Sun* (1961). "But He did give us children to make them dreams seem worthwhile." Those dreams may soon explode like fatal fireworks in a two-bedroom Chicago apartment that also houses Lena's thirty-five-year-old son, Walter Lee (Sidney Poitier); her college-age daughter, Beneatha (Diana Sands); and Walter Lee's wife, Ruth (Ruby Dee), and their son, Travis (Stephen Perry).

Beneatha, hoping to become a doctor, needs money to pursue her studies. Walter Lee, chafing at his chauffeur's job, hopes to start a business of his own, a liquor store, with some friends. Ruth, strapped for funds in a marriage grown cold, is pregnant with a second child she plans to abort. They all could use a chunk of Big Walter's $10,000 insurance policy. But Lena has her own mission: to move her family out of a ghetto flat and into a nice house in a white neighborhood. That means no investment in a business she disapproves of: Walter Lee's liquor store. "You butchered up a dream of mine," he cries. "You, mama, who's always talkin''bout her children's dreams."

Winner of the New York Drama Critics Circle award in 1959, *A Raisin in the Sun* made Lorraine Hansberry, twenty-eight, the first black woman to have a play on Broadway. She took her title from a Langston Hughes poem—which asks whether "a dream deferred" dries up "like a raisin in the sun?"—and the kernel of her plot from a lawsuit that her realtor father brought against racially segregated housing in Chicago (*Hansberry v. Lee*), which the Supreme Court decided in his favor in 1940. But the play and its faithful film version, with the original cast under Daniel Petrie's astute direction, contain echoes of other classic family parables and other powerful, burdened wives and mothers. Lena is like Ma Joad in *The Grapes of Wrath*, determined to move from the meager home she cherished to a future of uncertain hope. She could also be Linda Loman in *Death of a Salesman*, if Linda had believed in Willy's dream and tried to impose it on her grown sons after he died. Lena hasn't raised her family through war's battles and blitzes, but when the Youngers get a glimpse of their possible home in the suburbs, her children give her a straw hat with the dedication: "To our own Mrs. Miniver."

As much as Walter Lee and Beneatha love their mother, they also resent her clinging to the ways of her generation. Beneatha harbors all manner of advanced ideas, from black nationalism to modern dance, but when she declares herself an atheist, Lena slaps her hard and thunders, "Now you say after me: In my mother's house *there is still God.*" Walter Lee, the chauffeur-servant who wants to be a boss, bitterly proclaims, "I'm a volcano, I'm a giant, and I'm surrounded by ants!" Smoldering with a black man's aspirations, he feels he's treated like a child by the mother who often summons the memory of Big Walter to demean her son. ("I'm waiting to hear how you'd be like your father, be the man that he was.") Haunted and taunted, frustrated and emasculated, he finally assails Lena: "*You're* the head of this family! You run our lives the way you want, you spend the money the way you want." In this titanic war of wills, only Ruth can apply the balm of perspective. "You just got some strong-willed children," she tells her mother-in-law, "and it takes a strong woman like you to keep 'em in hand."

Juggling a half-dozen hot-button issues in a finely crafted problem play, Hansberry (who died of pancreatic cancer at thirty-four) never let agitprop overwhelm her flair for family drama; she gives each character compelling reasons for speaking up in pride and pain. The entire cast rises to the splendid occasion she created for them. Poitier, who took a year off from movie stardom to appear in the play, is the marquee name, but McNeil—just six and a half years older than the actor playing her son—is the dominant force. With an ample frame suggesting an urbanized, updated Hattie McDaniel, McNeil plants herself at the center of the screen and rarely yields the spatial foreground or moral high ground. In his memoir, *The Measure of an Actor: A Spiritual Autobiography*, Poitier recalls that McNeil "was in complete dominance over most of the other members of the cast." On the matter of whether the mother or the daughter should be the focus of the piece, "we argued constantly." Poitier might have skipped the debate and ceded preeminence to McNeil's grand, grounded performance. She makes Lena a mother with whom it would be a challenge and an honor to collide.

The first TV play to be expanded into a movie, *Marty* (1955), won four Oscars: Best Motion Picture, Director (Delbert Mann), Actor (Ernest Borgnine) and Screenplay (Paddy Chayefsky). In a decade when Hollywood was fighting the incursion of TV with, to quote the Cole Porter song from *Silk Stockings*, "glorious Technicolor, breathtaking CinemaScope and stereophonic sound," *Marty* signaled both a return to the black-and-white intimacy of thirties movies and a harbinger of the Sundance genre of indie films. It was a relationship dramedy about an ordinary guy—the thirty-four-year-old Bronx butcher Marty Piletti—with nothing

Marty, 1955: Esther Minciotti as Ernest Borgnine's comforting, confining mother.

but a friend (Joe Mantell), an eventual girlfriend (Betsy Blair) and a mother (Esther Minciotti), whom he lives with. He spends his days chopping meat and his weeknights with his pal Angie. Saturdays, at his mother's insistence, he goes to a local dance, looks for a nice girl and comes home alone, with defeat that nags like an impacted molar.

Marty, whose "charm lies in his almost indestructible good humor" (says Chayefsky in the script), and his mother are decent people with irreconcilable agitations; they could be a long-married couple whose arguments have become rituals. She wants him to find a nice girl; he thinks he can't. One Saturday evening at the kitchen table, Marty tries to explain his situation: "Sooner or later there comes a point in a man's life when he's gotta face some facts. And one fact I gotta face is that whatever it is that women like, I ain't got it. I chased enough girls in my life, I went to enough dances. I got hurt enough. I don't wanna get hurt no more. . . . I'm gonna stay home tonight and watch the *Hit Parade*." When his mother keeps pressing her case, the quiet man explodes: "I'm ugly, I'm ugly, I'm ugly—Ma, leave me alone!" Just as quickly, he subsides back into resignation. "All right," he says, "so I'll go to the Stardust Ballroom, I'll put on a blue suit and I'll go. And you know what I'm gonna get for my trouble? Heartache. A big night of heartache."

The scene's wellspring is excellent writing from Chayefsky, but it flows through Borgnine's precise and intuitive orchestration of emotion. He recognized that Marty has accepted his failure—a disease he's lived with so long he can diagnose it without getting upset—and that only when his mother pushes the point does he triphammer into rage. After his outburst, he sits down; pats his mother's hand twice, as if to say it's all right; and eats his spaghetti. (That was a Borgnine touch. As he told Robert Osborne during a TCM interview in 2009, "It's one of those gestures: I understand, Mom, that's how I feel.") So Marty won by making his mom realize he thinks he's a loser. But guess what? He's wrong, she's right, because later in the film, Miss Wonderful—or, in the Chayefsky universe of livable compromises, Miss Okay—is waiting for Mr. Ugly.

. . .

Hollywood quickly got the *Marty* message. Within three months of its Oscar victory, MGM released **The Catered Affair** (1956), another Bronx tale from a Chayefsky teleplay (adapted for movies by Gore Vidal) and starring Borgnine. This time, instead of Esther Minciotti as the woman of his house, the actor had Bette Davis. Borgnine is Tom Hurley, a cab driver who has nearly saved enough money to buy his own hack; Davis is his wife, Agnes Hurley, whom the decades have left about as chipper as a DMV drudge at the end of a horrible day. One morning, their daughter, Jane (Debbie Reynolds), tells them that she will be marrying her beau Ralph (Rod Taylor). Nothing fancy, just a quick service with the immediate family and no reception. But when Ralph's middle-class parents start bragging about the big weddings they gave their daughters, Aggie gets competitive, even as the guest list rises toward two hundred for what Tom calls "this criminal breakfast we're serving a bunch of strangers." Ready to plunder his taxi savings, Aggie tells Jane, "You're going to have a big wedding whether you like it or not. And if you don't like it, you don't have to come."

In the TV version, Thelma Ritter played Aggie. It requires a leap of faith, and fondness for the magnificent Bette, to believe that Davis's grand gestures can be shoehorned into a lumpen character in a tiny apartment. But under Richard Brooks's direction, she pushes Aggie past parody into a snapshot of bluster and defeat. As she makes the bed, Aggie offers Jane a mother's wisdom on wedded bliss: "Marriage is a big thing like some girls don't know nowadays. You gotta make sacrifices, and when the children start comin' you gotta put 'em first, ahead of everybody. . . . And then one day you'll find out a lotta time's gone by, and you wake up knowin' this is the way it's always gonna be, just like this, day after day, year after year, just the same. . . . And don't get married thinkin' it's only a good time. It's not a bad time but it's not a good time, livin' all your life with one man and strugglin' to raise the children decent." In a single spouting of autobiography masquerading as advice, Aggie has escalated from acidic realism to primal scream.

"If you've never been hated by your child," the real Davis once said, "you've never been a parent." (Her daughter B. D. Hyman published a memoir, *My Mother's Keeper*, after which the star disinherited her and her children.) As a mother, on-screen or off,

Davis might have been a handful, and in *The Catered Affair* Aggie's bitter whims test Jane's patience. Reynolds's smart tactic is to glide through the turmoil by ignoring it; she might be closing her eyes and picturing Mom as played by Mary Astor. Jane knows that the wedding is something she doesn't need or want but her mother does. Decades earlier, Aggie's father had offered Tom $300 to marry her. She has held up her end of the connubial contract dutifully but not warmly; when she slips out of her dress, she tells her husband to "turn around." And now, with Jane leaving, she and Tom will be alone together for the first time. No wonder the sour, stoic Aggie collapses in sobs—and why, when discovered, she shrugs and says, "Well, that was a dumb thing to do." A lady, especially a movie queen in a Bronx tenement, has to salvage her dignity.

Having imagined Debbie Reynolds as the child of Ernest Borgnine and Bette Davis, you must now picture Reynolds, forty years later, as the mother of Albert Brooks. Who could the father have been—Albert Einstein? (Which happens to be Brooks's birth name.) In ***Mother*** (1996), the actor-director-cowriter plays John Henderson, devastated and impoverished by the failure of his second marriage. Years before the trend of America's adult children moving back in with their folks exploded into a societal phenomenon, John decides to return home. By staying with his widowed mother Beatrice (Reynolds), he thinks he will be able to unearth the root of his problems with women. It's as if he figured that therapy would be more successful if he lived with his shrink—or, rather, with the person who made him feel he needed a shrink.

Beatrice isn't sold on the idea; she's accommodated herself to the single life, and to a man friend. ("We're not intimate, dear," she tells her son. "We just have sex occasionally.") And she pretty clearly is disappointed in John: she introduces him to her

facing page: The Catered Affair, 1956: Bette Davis eyes her bride-to-be daughter, Debbie Reynolds.

Mother, 1996: Debbie Reynolds has a maternal issue—son Albert Brooks.

friends as "my other son." But he moves back into his old bedroom, with the furnishings of his youth, to promote his DIY psychotherapy. Often he acts as Beatrice's analyst. She says, "I love you, John"; he replies, "I know you think you do, Mother." The odd couple argues over food: his organic and fresh, hers generic and years old. Scanning her refrigerator, which he calls "a food museum," he tries some frozen sherbet in what she says is its "protective ice coating." One bite, and he observes, "This tastes like an orange *foot*." All right, so culinary habits evolved from Beatrice's prime to John's. That's how they eventually find solace: by understanding that two people are different, even or especially if one gave birth to the other. In her first starring role in a quarter century, Reynolds infused Beatrice with a delicate comic underplaying—organic, not generic—that lets the viewer decide if this mother was right or wrong, or just a woman trying to remember what she loved about her amiably neurotic son.

"She respects me, but she doesn't want to become like me," says Jane Fonda of her daughter in Neil Simon's *California Suite* (1978). "We have a perfectly normal mother-daughter relationship." In the 1976 **Freaky Friday**, mother Ellen (Barbara Harris) and daughter Annabel (Jodie Foster) did become each other, for a day, by simultaneously shouting a magic curse. A progenitor of body-switch comedies, Mary Rodgers's book and screenplay also gave pert prominence to the distinction of family roles: the mother burdened by domestic chores, the tween girl with a carefree life she thinks is indentured servitude. The humor, befitting a Disney film, is carefree and laundered: Annabel as Ellen calls her father/husband "Daddy," and, since she's in charge of cooking, prepares a rum-raisin banana-split breakfast. She should move in with Debbie Reynolds's Beatrice.

The 2003 remake, in a snider time for movie comedy, manages the same easy, mostly sexless fantasy, this time with Jamie Lee Curtis as Tess, the mother, and the momentarily adorable Lindsay Lohan as Anna, the kid. One generation's scandal is the next one's rite of passage, as when Tess, in Anna's body, realizes her daughter had her navel pierced. And Anna is shocked to pinch her flesh and realize she's old, "like the Crypt Keeper." The mild satirical point is that we are what we are even when we

Freaky Friday, 1976: Jodie Foster and Barbara Harris endure a one-day body switch.

look like someone else. Says Tess-Anna to Anna-Tess, "When you get your body back, you're grounded."

A woman with a teenage or adult child has to acknowledge, at least implicitly, a challenge to her own youth and sex appeal. Some mothers get the message early, like Charlotte Haze in Stanley Kubrick's 1962 film of the Vladimir Nabokov novel ***Lolita***. Charlotte may thrust her charms under the nose of visiting scholar Humbert Humbert (James Mason), but one look at the fourteen-year-old Lo (Sue Lyon) in her skimpy bikini, with her downy skin and a vixen's smile, obliterates all thoughts of mature womanhood in Humbert the besotted nympholept.

facing page: Freaky Friday, 2003: Lindsay Lohan and Jamie Lee Curtis take on the roles of Foster and Harris—and Harris and Foster.

Lolita, 1962: Shelley Winters concentrates on ignoring the affection her daughter, Sue Lyon, betrays for the new boarder, James Mason.

A telling satire on, among many topics, the American worship of youth as it blossomed in the 1950s, *Lolita* pushes its point by encasing Charlotte, whom the Nabokov novel describes as "a weak solution of Marlene Dietrich," in the zaftig shrillness of Shelley Winters. Viewers may not share Humbert's taste for underage flesh, but they may be as glad to see Winters meet her watery end here (thunderstorm, speeding car) as they were to see Montgomery Clift drown her in *A Place in the Sun*.

Mother-daughter resentment over good looks is even pricklier when the older woman is the dish, the younger the dishrag. In ***The Mirror Has Two Faces*** (1996), Columbia professor Rose Morgan (Barbra Streisand) feels totally out-glammed by her pretty sister Claire (Mimi Rogers) and their haughty, resplendent mother, Hannah (Lauren Bacall), who presses her advantage by telling Rose to put on some makeup. Rose: "I *am* wearing makeup," adding, "What's the point? I'll still look like me, only in color." Rose soon gets her Bette Davis–in–*Now, Voyager* makeover and her all-but-ideal husband (Jeff Bridges). She also gets to make up with her mother. In a lovely scene shared by two generations of Jewish movie queens—the forties cover girl Bacall and the sixties sensation Streisand—Rose asks, "How did it feel to be beautiful?" Hannah's reply: "It was *wonderful!*" At that moment, the mean parent is humanized, as Rose realizes that most mothers, like most people, have their own memories, dreams and regrets.

Mildred Pierce, 1945: Joan Crawford slaves her way to success for her thankless child, Ann Blyth.

BAD SEEDS

What's a mother to do when she senses
something terribly wrong in the child she loves?

"How sharper than a serpent's tooth," keened King Lear, "it is to have a thankless child." He was speaking of Cordelia, the one of his three daughters who loved him enough to tell him the bleak truth, and the only one to accompany the monarch on his journey into madness. Whereas Lear misread his good daughter, some movie mothers are blinded by love from realizing, until too late, the devious minds behind their children's seraphic faces.

The trickle of evil-kid movies became a flood after the success of 1978's *Halloween*, which begins with a mother discovering that her adorable eight-year-old son has just slashed his sister to bits. But even in its more decorous golden age, Hollywood occasionally made films about children who were thankless, soulless, rotten to the core or simply unable to do the right thing by a mother's love. Here be monsters—underage sociopaths. And—if we look in the mirror of our last example, *Make Way for Tomorrow*—here we may be.

On his *Campbell Playhouse* broadcast of October 29, 1939, Orson Welles described Booth Tarkington's 1918 novel ***The Magnificent Ambersons*** as "the truest, cruelest picture of the growth of the Middle West, and the liveliest portrait left to us of the people who made it grow." In its tale of two intertwined dynasties, the upstart Morgans and the old-money Ambersons, Welles's 1942 film version contrasted the go-getter grace of early-twentieth-century entrepreneurs with the dissolution, the spread of ethical and emotional flab, of a young man born to wealth. "True" would describe this story of a son who sabotages his mother's one chance for happiness; "cruel" the film's fate at the scissors of the RKO executives who had sponsored Welles's previous effort, *Citizen Kane*; and "lively" *Ambersons'* sustained grip, even in its mutilated form, on audiences today.

"Old money" in Indianapolis meant three generations. Major Amberson (Richard Bennett) had created the family fortune by "buying and building and trading and banking," by fighting and conniving for it, employing brains and elbows and possibly fists. Was the major a robber baron? His grandson George Amberson Minafer only assumes he was a baron, an American monarch, which must make George a royal—if only a royal pain. His mother, Isabel (Dolores Costello), a sad beauty who loved the upstart Eugene Morgan (Joseph Cotten), instead married the middle-class cipher Wilbur Minafer (Don Dillaway). George, the only child of that drab marriage, is unlovely and unloving but not unloved. Indeed, his mother has lavished all her devotion on him—too much—and in the scorching sun of her indulgence, he spoils.

A "girlie-cutie" in ringlets, young George had been a spiteful prig: the townspeople couldn't wait for the day "when that boy would get his comeuppance." At first, Eugene tried to overlook George's faults: "Oh, he's still only a boy. Plenty of fine stuff in him. Can't help but be. He's Isabel Amberson's son." That's ardor trumping evidence. In fact, George more closely resembles Wilbur's spinster sister Fanny (Agnes Moorehead), who secretly loved Eugene and, when ignored, poured her poison into her nephew. By his college years, George's unchecked privilege has calcified into contempt for everyone less lucky (or, as he thinks, less worthy) than he. It will fester into envy of Eugene: of the older man's success as a manufacturer of automobiles, and of the love that Eugene and Isabel share—the film's one pure connection. Eugene's daughter, Lucy (Anne Baxter), who inherited her father's good sense and pacific poise, might have offered George the lifeline of her affection, if only his vision weren't occluded by moral myopia, if only he would stop insulting her father and his business. "Automobiles!" he spits out as an expletive to the startled Lucy. "People aren't going to spend their lives lying on their backs in the road letting grease drip in their faces."

As the mechanical marvel of motion pictures displaced the stage in bringing narrative myths to the public, so did cars replace carriages; they signaled the freedom of Americans to go where and when they wanted. Economically, that mobility was also vertical, spurring Eugene's wealth while the Amberson fortune is sapped by George's profligacy. The older man is the gleaming technological future; the younger, the crumbling aristocratic past. George, who disdains all professions, from lawyers and bankers to tinker-mechanics like Eugene, tells Lucy he plans to be "a yachtsman." But his real career, his one mission, will be to keep his mother for himself and away from Eugene. Raised as the sole object of her love, he won't admit that anyone else can occupy her heart.

In a letter to Isabel, Eugene finally dares to address her misshapen maternal bond. "Oh, dearest woman in the world, I know what your son is to you and it frightens me. . . . Will you live your life your way, or George's way? Dear, it breaks my heart for you, but what you have to oppose now is your own selfless and perfect motherhood. Are you strong enough, Isabel? Can you make a fight?" She cannot. She takes a European holiday with George, which he prolongs as her health ebbs. By the time they return, she is near death, and again George refuses Eugene's request to visit his beloved. (Her dying words: "I'd like to have seen him. Just once.") Let Eugene be the inventor; George has a unique gift for destruction. By the end he might agree that he killed his mother.

On the *Campbell Playhouse* radiocast of *Ambersons*, Welles had played George. Perhaps Welles thought he would squeeze too much of his grand, wastrel charm into the George role on film; the twenty-six-year-old actor-director's outsize showmanship might have won some sympathy for this agent of malice and misery. He gave the part to Tim Holt, a twenty-two-year-old cowboy star with a thin voice and no hint of screen charisma. Holt drove home the theme that a small personality, pursuing narrow vindictiveness, can bring down a great house. In some of the film's many elegant long-take long shots, Welles plants Holt just off center screen in a family debate; yet George's meanness dominates the action, because his mother and the other characters are too weak to challenge his viperous will.

Departing for Latin America to research his next project, *It's All True*, Welles left behind his 132-minute *Ambersons*. Then another family crime occurred. After a poorly received preview screening, the George Minafers at RKO cut fully a third of the film, down to 88 minutes. They then destroyed the excised footage, confounding all attempts at restoration. (In 2002, director Alfonso Arau shot Welles's screenplay for an *Ambersons* TV movie. Starring Madeleine Stowe as Isabel, Bruce Greenwood as Eugene and Jonathan Rhys Meyers as George, it ran 139 minutes.) From a mistaken form of love for her son, Isabel had criminally spoiled him. From the frantic desperation to carve a marketable commodity out of Welles's second masterpiece, the RKO executives turned the Amberson property into its own ruined, haunted mansion. Like the demolition crew at the end of *Citizen Kane*, they consigned precious footage to the flames, saying, in effect, "Throw that junk in."

Mildred Pierce (Joan Crawford) had one nice daughter: Kay (Jo Ann Marlowe). But this pert tomboy, who wanted to be a dancer, died of pneumonia at ten. In the 1945 **Mildred Pierce**, from the James

M. Cain novel, Kay's death leaves the bereaved mother with her elder daughter, Veda (Ann Blyth), the very definition of thanklessness. Veda might have admired Mildred—the family's sole support after the departure of her shiftless husband Bert (Bruce Bennett)—for working hard to give her the material bounty she never had. That is the American ethos: parents strive so their children can thrive. Veda, though, has the snobbish airs of a girl born to wealth; she could be George Minafer transplanted from turn-of-the-century Indianapolis to 1940s Glendale, California. Mildred, in her voice-over narration, calls her "a young lady with expensive tastes." Translation: ungrateful bitch.

The mild contempt that Veda ladled on her kid sister ("You act like a peasant," she told Kay) ripens to venom against her mother. When she learns that Mildred's job is waitressing, she explodes—"Did you have to degrade us?"—ignoring the elementary math that the cash Mildred earns buys the new home, clothes and status that Veda thinks she deserves. Mildred's keen entrepreneurship—buying a roadside property from playboy Monte Beragon (Zachary Scott) and expanding it to a flourishing chain of restaurants—brings them wealth, but Veda wants to be more than moneyed. She wants to be *old money*, with its attendant luxe and dissolution. Another American story: children take for granted the gifts their parents struggled to lavish on them; they resent the grimy grind that produced the largesse. To Veda, the polo-playing idler Monte represents wealth unsullied by labor. "I want the kind of life that Monte taught me," she tells Mildred, "and you won't give it to me."

Veda can never forgive her mother for making money the old-fashioned way: by earning it. The girl has a simpler route to her own wealth: she becomes engaged to a rich young man, then takes money from his family to walk away. That check finances Veda's dreams of escape. "With this money I can get away from you," she tells Mildred in a memorably serpentine soliloquy. "From you and your chickens and your pies and your kitchens and everything that smells of grease. I can get away from this shack with its cheap furniture, and this town and its dollar days, and its women that wear uniforms and its men that wear overalls." She hates the working class, but not as much as she despises the mother who rose from it. "You think just because you made a little money you can get a new hairdo and some expensive clothes and turn yourself into a lady. But you can't, because you'll never be anything but a common frump whose father lived over a grocery store and whose mother took in washing. With this money I can get away from every rotten, stinking thing that makes me think of this place or you." Mildred tears up the check, slaps Veda and throws her out.

Broke but independent, Veda takes a job singing at a nightclub dive; when Mildred sees this, her face freezes in shame—in a generational flip of the scene in *Applause* where Helen Morgan performs in a burlesque house with her abashed daughter in the audience. (In 1957, Blyth would star in the Warners biopic *The Helen Morgan Story*.) And still Mildred wants Veda's love and respect. In her most cynical transaction, Mildred offers Monte one-third of the restaurant business to marry her—"Sold, one Beragon"—and buys a new house with a picture of the young Veda atop the grand piano. Veda's brief return and honeyed words ("I'll never say mean things to you again") brings tears to Mildred's eyes. She will cry again when she discovers that Veda wants one more thing Mildred owns: Monte.

Ranald MacDougall's script adds the framing device of a murder to the Cain novel (to whose plot particulars Todd Haynes adhered much more faithfully in his five-and-a-half-hour HBO miniseries in 2011), and director Michael Curtiz imprisons the characters in the rhomboidal architecture of film noir shadows. Crawford, who won the Best Actress Oscar in her first Warners movie after sixteen years at MGM, should be the dominant figure, sporting career-woman jackets with the shoulder pads of an NFL lineman and radiating the nobility of an ardent mother who, like another of Shakespeare's tragic heroes, "loved not wisely, but too well." Yet it's Blyth who corrals the viewer's appalled fascination. From her doll's face come the most heinous words a mother could hear, including her climactic plea: "Give me another chance. It's your fault I'm the way I am." Veda has decided that, if she's bad, her mother must be the seed.

"Oh, I've got the *prettiest* mother," eight-year-old Rhoda Penmark (Patty McCormack) purrs in a metallic singsong at the start of the 1956 film *The Bad Seed*. And Christine Penmark (Nancy Kelly) has the nastiest

The Bad Seed, 1956: Nancy Kelly and her pigtailed predator, Patty McCormack.

daughter. An icon of midcentury wholesomeness in blond pigtails with a chirpy voice to charm grownups, Rhoda seems miffed that her classmate Claude won the penmanship medal she coveted but, later, is unfazed at the news of Claude's death at a school picnic. Christine is mystified, but the creepy janitor Leroy (Henry Jones) knows a vicious kid when he sees one. Taunting Rhoda about the missing medal, he says that the state executes children who murder: "They got a little blue chair for little boys and a little pink chair for little gals." (Leroy's intuitive sleuthing will earn him a fiery demise in the basement furnace.) When Christine finds the medal, she confronts Rhoda. "Do you realize that you murdered him?" "But it was his fault!" Psychopathy always has an excuse.

Trailers for the movie implored audiences to keep its secret: not that Rhoda is elfin evil in a pinafore dress, which is evident from reel one, but that her malignancy may be inherited. (Christine is horrified to learn that her actual mother was a serial killer, Bessie Denker, and infers that the bad seed skipped a generation, from Bessie to Rhoda.) William March's 1954 novel and the play adaptation of the same year by Maxwell Anderson both ended with Christine's suicide and Rhoda's survival. The Hollywood Production Code allowed murder but insisted on retribution, so in director Mervyn LeRoy's studiously stagey film version, which reunited virtually all of the original Broadway cast, Christine survives, and Rhoda returns to the site of Claude's death, where God's lightning strikes her down. (In a 2004 interview, McCormack recalls that, as a good Catholic girl, she had prayed to get the Rhoda role. God answered her prayers too.) For good measure, the movie summons the actors for a curtain call. Kelly, the last to appear, bends McCormack over her knee and gives her a severe spanking, as if a good mother could beat the devil out of a killer child.

Bad kids: where do they come from? Hollywood films had invested so much narrative capital in the idealizing of the American family—in ancestry as destiny—that they did handsprings when they had to justify the source of childhood monstrosity. George Minafer? The product of a loveless marriage and a mother's thoughtless worship. Veda Pierce? Her lazy father, Bert, was just as dependent on, and dismissive of, Mildred's efforts to support the family. Rhoda Penmark? Like grandmother, like granddaughter.

Melodrama resides in the far corners of most people's experience. Audiences can distance themselves from genre excesses with a shiver or a shrug, saying, "Well, *my* mother wasn't a serial killer." It's the rare film, touching issues closer to home, that burrows into the collective conscience and gives a moviegoer more chills and squirms than any homicidal child could. Perhaps that is why so few of these films get made. The 1937 film ***Make Way for Tomorrow***, directed by Leo McCarey from Viña Delmar's screenplay, addresses two uncomfortable, unavoidable topics—the struggles of the middle class in the Great Depression, and the responsibility that adult children owe to their parents—and does so with judicious grace. What Welles said of Tarkington's *Ambersons* applies here: the movie manages to be simultaneously cruel, lively and true.

The title sounds chipper; it could be the billboard slogan for some lustrous planned community. But to Lucy (Beulah Bondi) and Barkley Cooper (Victor Moore), married for a half century, "Make way for tomorrow" has a dictatorial air, as in: get out of the way for the next generation—you old folks are yesterday. Bark, a bookkeeper, has been out of work for four years, and now the bank has foreclosed on the house where he and Lucy raised their five children. At a family conference, the eldest son, George (Thomas Mitchell), and his wife, Anita (Fay Bainter), agree to take Lucy into their Manhattan apartment, sharing a room with their teenage daughter Rhoda (Barbara Read), while Bark will sleep on the couch in the small-town home of daughter Cora (Elizabeth Risdon) and her husband Bill (Ralph Remley), who is also out of work. Though it might seem thoughtless, separating the single organism that Barkley and Lucy have grown into, their children have limited space and means, and their own lives to lead. The chain of family obligations goes down the generations, not back up. As Bark says, "I sometimes think that children should never grow past the age when you have to tuck 'em into bed every night."

In short order, Lucy gets on the nerves of her hosts as much as the squeaks from her rocking chair. Her nattering presence drives Rhoda's young friends away from visiting the apartment. She disrupts a bridge class Anita teaches in the living room and upsets the players with her side of a phone call from Bark, which ends with Lucy promising, "We'll soon be together always." She already suspects that is a fantasy; George has been receiving mail from the Idylwild Home for Aged Women. In a beautiful scene, Lucy anticipates her son's plan by insisting that she go to the home. But George mustn't tell Bark: "It'll be the first secret I've ever had from him." Bark is also being moved, to another daughter out in California—for health reasons, the exasperated Cora proclaims. He and Lucy get one last day together, in Manhattan, where they rekindle their love, far from the children to whom they have become such a bother. "I guess this is the first time away from home together since our honeymoon," Bark notes. And their last.

The movie validates the testimony of the great French auteur Jean Renoir that "Leo McCarey understood people better than any other Hollywood director." The Japanese screenwriter Kogo Noda recognized the knotty human elements in *Make Way for Tomorrow* and wrote the script for a similarly poignant tale of aged parents and busy children: Yasujiro Ozu's 1953 masterpiece **Tokyo Story**. Some critics have charged McCarey, who won Best Director Oscars for screwball comedy (*The Awful Truth*) and uplifting priestly drama (*Going My Way*), with ruthless sentimentalism. *Make Way for Tomorrow*, though, is a spectacular balancing act of humor and dread. Yes, the movie opens with a rendition of "Mother"—"'M' is for the million things she gave me; / 'O' means only that she's growing old"—and closes with "Let Me Call You Sweetheart." But the first song is meant sarcastically and the second as an elegy for two people, together forever, now parting. Earlier, Lucy says of a movie she saw that it's "a little sad in places, but it had a happy ending." *Make Way for Tomorrow* is a little sad and a little funny, but it dares to follow its narrative logic to a wrenching conclusion.

McCarey allows some jokes at the grown kids' expense, as when a friendly stranger hears that Bark and Lucy have five children, saying, "I'll bet they brought you a lot of pleasure," and Bark replies, "I bet you haven't any children." Toward the end, Robert (Ray Mayer), the mild scoundrel of the siblings, pronounces stern judgment on the grown children when he observes, "We've known all along that we're probably the most good-for-nothing bunch of kids that were ever raised. But it didn't

Tokyo Story, 1953: two aging parents (Chishû Ryû,
Chieko Higashiyama), one dutiful daughter (Setsuko Hara).

bother us much until we found out that Pop knew it too." The children have behaved selfishly, or at least clumsily, toward their parents, but this is a film of nuances, not extremes; of no real villains, only victims. And no final catharsis. Moviegoers may feel a momentary cleansing when a wicked child gets her comeuppance in *Mildred Pierce* or *The Bad Seed*. But some real-life dilemmas elude easy solutions. Such as: Where do people go between old age and death? And: Should grown children disrupt their lives for the parents who sacrificed theirs?

Now Voyager, 1942: A malicious Boston matriarch (Gladys Cooper) schemes
to ensure that the life of her daughter (Bette Davis) is a Vale of tears.

MALEVOLENT MOMS

An actress's fast route to Oscar nominations: playing rotten mothers. Throw these mommas from the train!

Bad mothers: you know they're out there. Not you, dear reader, or your mom. Sweet and spotless, we're sure. But the law of averages would argue that, among the billions of women who have given birth and raised kids, a few must be really rotten. From misguided notions of the maternal bond, a woman may become a dominating, domineering mother. Or avarice may drive her to propose a marriage between her daughter and her first cousin, and to allow her husband to die without treatment (Bette Davis's Regina Giddens in *The Little Foxes*). Perhaps she wishes to assert her own youthfulness by initiating an affair with the young neighbor who will become her daughter's boyfriend (Anne Bancroft as Mrs. Robinson in *The Graduate*). Or she exercises power, not affection, over her child, until and after she dies (Judi Dench in *J. Edgar*).

Some of these sins stain the four mothers in this chapter. Mrs. Vale in **Now, Voyager** may be imposing a literal meaning on the old verse "A son's a son till he takes a wife; a daughter's a daughter the rest of her life"; she treats her daughter as an unloved maid. Mrs. Phelps in *The Silver Cord* extends that truism to her two sons. Needing love, she takes it, drains it from them, and cripples them by refusing, when they're grown, to treat them as adults with their own wills and passions. Mrs. Iselin in *The Manchurian Candidate* uses her son to terrorist political ends. (Note that the mothers in all three films are not referred to by their first names; each is a "Mrs.," a widow concentrating her twisted energies on her children.) In *Precious*, Mary Johnston prostitutes her daughter to hold on to her man—the girl's father.

As goodness can reveal nobility, evil can display grandeur. Medea, the queen who killed her children, was a tragic figure and an object lesson in Euripides's fifth-century B.C. play. Played by Maria Callas in Pier Paolo Pasolini's 1969 film, she is an otherworldly eminence—a ghost whose nature and duty it is to bring the living to death. Twenty-five hundred years of drama have verified the lasting lure of wicked women. And by tracing the descent of "bad mothers" into ignominy, the actresses who play them rise in stature. "Some of my most interesting roles have been completely unsympathetic," Barbara Stanwyck said in the late 1940s. "Actresses welcome such parts, knowing that vitriol makes a stronger impression than syrup." Audiences know that too. We may deplore bad movie mothers, but they lure us into their webs.

NOW, VOYAGER . . .

This is the movie where a man lights two cigarettes and gives one to the woman he loves—back when smoking was cool. It's the film where Bette Davis's Charlotte Vale transforms herself from spinster to bombshell by dropping twenty-five pounds, choosing a livelier couture, trading sensible shoes for stylish ones, taking off her glasses and tweezing her eyebrows. Casey Robinson's screenplay, from the third in Olive Higgins Prouty's quintet of Vale novels, packs in mother hatred, adoptive-mother love, three nervous breakdowns, two ill-starred engagements, an adulterous affair, a messily platonic relationship and a huge, rich, hostile family. This 1942 tightrope walk above a tub of scalding bathos is also, arguably, the best movie directed by anyone named Irving. Last name: Rapper.

But as potent as is the smoldering, erotic glow of passion and nicotine between Charlotte and Paul Henreid's Jerry Durrance, and a Max Steiner score that samples Tchaikovsky's grandly romantic Symphony No. 6, the film is also a scathing portrait of maternal possessiveness. Mrs. Henry Vale holds her only daughter's life and potential happiness in a death grip. And Gladys Cooper (who, like Davis, was Oscar-nominated for her performance) embodies her as a severe, sepulchral creature with gray hair in a bun—like a better-dressed, slightly more animated but no less vindictive Mother Bates. Mother Vale has kept Charlotte a virtual prisoner in their Boston mansion since the girl was twenty and dared to fall in love with a man not of her class. Now Charlotte is nearly twice that age, and still, she tells the amiable psychiatrist Dr. Jaquith (Claude Rains), "I am my mother's well-loved daughter [this with sarcasm]. I am her companion. I am my mother's servant. My mother! My *mother*!" Charlotte won't challenge the Vale virago, but Jaquith will: "[Charlotte] is most seriously ill, thanks to you. My dear Mrs. Vale, if you had deliberately and maliciously planned to destroy your daughter's life, you couldn't have done it more completely."

In believing that the frumpy, withdrawn Charlotte could never attract a husband, Mrs. Vale could be a New England cousin of another plutocrat with a homely daughter, Austin Sloper in Henry James's *Washington Square* (filmed in 1949 as *The Heiress*, with Ralph Richardson and Olivia de Havilland). A parent's contempt is reflected in her child's shattered self-image. But Mrs. Vale's true meanness resides in the grim pleasure she takes in imposing her steel will on her only daughter. She has ruined Charlotte out of rancor and for sport.

After her recovery in Jaquith's sanatorium and her shipboard affair with Jerry, the transformed Charlotte is prepared to live at home as her mother's equal. ("Remember that whatever she may have done," Jaquith advises, "she's your mother.")

To Mrs. Vale, though, the new Charlotte is a threat to her domestic despotism. She insists that Charlotte doff the Orry-Kelly gowns and don the old frump attire. "As to your hair and eyebrows," she piquantly adds, "you can say that often after a severe illness one loses one's hair, but you're letting yours grow as quickly as possible." Charlotte cannot be surprised that her mother demands the status quo. Yet something has changed: Charlotte is no longer afraid of her.

Bad mothers in movies often say they wish their child had died. Mrs. Vale pushes that curse into derision: "I should think you'd be ashamed to be born and live all your life as Charlotte Vale. *Miss* Charlotte Vale." By now, Charlotte's external and internal makeover gives her confidence to fight back: "Dr. Jaquith says that tyranny is sometimes an expression of the maternal instinct. If that's a mother's love, I want no part of it. I didn't want to be born. You didn't want me to be born either. It's been a calamity on both sides." Stricken by her daughter's bold veracity, Mrs. Vale has a heart attack and dies. Charlotte blames herself: "We quarreled. I did it." Only a good daughter would feel so guilty. Yet after an earlier argument her mother had tumbled down the Vale staircase, risking killing herself just to spite Charlotte. Now she is dead, and with the added malediction of leaving her substantial fortune to Charlotte, she means to haunt her decent daughter forever. Mrs. Vale's bony hands claw at her from the grave.

THE SILVER CORD

"You'll love Mother, she's marvelous," David Phelps (Joel McCrea) tells his bride Christina (Irene Dunne). In fact, Mrs. Phelps (Laura Hope Crews) is a marvel of scheming, suffocating possessiveness; she makes Mrs. Vale seem liberal by comparison. But whereas Charlotte's mother ruled with a tyrant's icy hauteur, Mrs. Phelps in **The Silver Cord** (1933) is jovial, when it suits her, and doting, to a fault. She employs flutter and bluster to shackle her grown sons David and Robert (Eric Linden) and divert outsiders. Christina is a gifted scientist who has returned from Germany to the States to work at the Rockefeller Institute—an appointment Mrs. Phelps dismisses by observing airily that "science is hardly a profession, is it? It's more of a hobby." She then assigns the new husband and wife to separate bedrooms.

In her close adaptation of Sidney Howard's 1926 play, screenwriter Jane Murfin focuses on how the apron strings of a strong woman can strangle her weak sons. Telling Robert, "Sit down—no, no, head in my lap," for an oddly erotic Pietà, Mrs. Phelps persuades him to break off his engagement to Hester (Frances Dee) and seals the deal with the malevolent-mother tactic of kissing him on the mouth. (See *The Manchurian Candidate*.) Later she tucks David into his solitary bed, sits on it, holds his hand and continues her dulcet plotting against Christina. Neither mama's boy—the effeminate Robert or the rugged-looking David—is a match for her. Robert declares that he broke up with Hester because of "the ideal of womankind that Mother gave us both by being the great woman that she is." Christina, who is pregnant, probes David about his mother's hold on him, and "what she may not do with you—to me, and the baby." Yet he remains myopic, saying, "A man's mother's his mother." (As in: the rest of his life.) "And what's his wife?" asks Christina, who comes to the sickening belief that she's "going to have a baby by a man who belongs to another woman."

Let us consider Mrs. Phelps's side for a moment. Her battle with Christina may in part be one of their respective generations; the cozy ideals of one age often seem antediluvian to the next. Christina is a modern, indeed pioneering, career woman; she seconds Hester's notion of raising children: "Have 'em, love 'em and then leave 'em be." Mrs. Phelps, raised in an earlier century, makes an eloquent plea for stay-at-home moms. "Give us our due, Christina. We weren't altogether bustles and smelling salts, we girls who did not go out into the world. We made a great profession, which I fear is in some danger of vanishing from the face of the earth. We made a profession of motherhood. That may sound old-fashioned to you. Believe me, it had its value."

It had, and has. But Mrs. Phelps distorted that value when she transferred the passion missing from her marriage to her sons. Widowed at twenty-five, she effectively became her boys' mother and wife. Any woman to whom David and Robert might feel romantic attraction earned the designation of a home wrecker, the Other Woman. "And I do not deny," she tells Christina, "that I'd cut off my right hand and burn the sight out of my eyes to rid my son of you." In this singeing five-character drama, which deserves to be rescued from obscurity, the main combatants are three strong women; the men are their puny pawns. Crews, reprising her Broadway role under John Cromwell's direction (he staged both the play and the film), reveals Mrs. Phelps's depredation artfully, gradually, like the slow opening of a Venus flytrap. But the movie allows the two modern women to render stern judgment on maternal love turned rancid. Christina: "You're not fit to be anyone's mother." And Hester, as she walks out of this nest of near-incest: "I'm going to marry an orphan!"

THE MANCHURIAN CANDIDATE

"My boys, my two boys," she says with a smile, hugging her son and her husband. "That's all I've ever cared about." Her second husband is Johnny Iselin (James Gregory), a U.S. senator in the 1950s Red-baiting mold, who uses a Heinz ketchup label to determine the number of Communists he insists are in the State Department. Her son, Johnny's stepson, is Raymond Shaw (Laurence Harvey), a Cold War cold-fish misfit who quite systematically kills eight people and, in the twisted political and domestic world of *The Manchurian Candidate* (1962), turns out to be the hero. And Mrs. Iselin (Angela Lansbury), whom Johnny calls "Babe" and Raymond "Mother"—which he pronounces as if expectorating a toad—is the complete villainous package: Joe McCarthy's puppeteer, the Red menace and the would-be assassin of a presidential candidate. Frank Sinatra and Janet Leigh also appear in the movie, as two of the three top-billed stars, but Lansbury and Harvey provide the central tension of two exceptional, odious creatures: a mother and her son whom genetics and geopolitics have consigned to a death match.

Writer George Axelrod and director John Frankenheimer's surreal, pertinent, acerbically comic film version of Richard Condon's multi-conspiracy novel proposes the view that America's most rabid anti-Communists were in cahoots with the Kremlin. Johnny is a secret Soviet agent, and Raymond, during his service in the Korean War, was brainwashed by Moscow and Peking to follow their murderous instructions whenever he hears a code phrase about card playing. The next time he hears it, his mission will be to shoot and kill this year's presidential nominee and thus sweep Senator Iselin—the Manchurian candidate—into the White House with, as Johnny's boss and Raymond's controller prophesizes, "powers that will make martial

law seem like anarchy." We don't know the identity of the American Soviet boss until Mrs. Iselin says to Raymond, "Why don't you pass the time by playing a little solitaire?"

In Lansbury's exquisite, audacious performance, which earned her an Oscar nomination and deserved more, Mrs. Iselin becomes both a ruthless, ingenious manipulator of realpolitik and, in her way, a victim. For her allies abroad also control *her*; they turned the son she may somehow love into the instrument of death she needs to use. In her last speech to Raymond she says, "I told them to build me an assassin. I wanted a killer from a world filled with killers, and they chose you because they thought it would bind me closer to them." She cradles Raymond's face in her hands. "But now, we have come almost to the end. One last step. And then when I take power, they will be pulled down and ground into dirt for what they did to you—and what they did in so contemptuously underestimating me." Then she gives her son a big slimy smooch on the lips; mother love never seemed so despotic or desperate.

Lansbury was just thirty-six during the filming, Harvey thirty-three (his first two wives were, respectively, six and seventeen years older than he). The actor's reptilian sangfroid makes him the perfect mom-hating son—and until nearly the end he doesn't know half of her capacity for evil. In the Mrs. Iselin character, Lansbury goes farther, darker and deeper: she invests a mother's love, a lover's passion and a killer's calculation in the Raymond relationship. Whatever Mrs. Iselin's defining political motives, that kiss is a satanic promise that no one, no nation or ideology, can ruin her son without tasting this mother's vengeance.

PRECIOUS: BASED ON THE NOVEL "PUSH" BY SAPPHIRE

Claireece Precious Jones (Gabourey Sidibe) is an illiterate, grossly obese sixteen-year-old with a wildly abusive mother, Mary (Mo'Nique), and a vagrant father who comes home only to rape his daughter. He has just impregnated the girl for the second time; her first child—dubbed Mongo, for Mongoloid—is brain-damaged and stays with Precious's grandmother. Word of the girl's pregnancy has led to her suspension from junior high school and threatens the family's eligibility for the welfare checks that are their only support. Precious's life is an unrelenting hell, and when a well-meaning soul suggests that things may be looking up, she tartly replies, "I'm lookin' up. Lookin' for a piano to fall. A desk, a couch, TV. My mom, maybe." Mary Johnston is the all-time most vile, deplorable, eye-magnetizing monster movie mother: Momzilla.

The novel *Push* by Sapphire (Ramona Lofton) updated the woeful early life of Celie, protagonist of Alice Walker's *The Color Purple*, from the early-twentieth-century American South to modern Harlem. Like the book, the film made in 2009, scripted by Geoffrey Fletcher and directed by Lee Daniels, is a horror story that becomes a hymn to the transformative effects of schooling. In this nearly all-female saga, Precious finds someone, Ms. Rain (Paula Patton), who gives her time, her passion and, best of all, a sense of hope to the poor kids in her care; she incarnates the view that a good teacher can be the best mother. As demonized as Ms. Rain is idealized, Mary Johnston bends her own talents for abuse to verbal and physical torrents against her daughter. In one tirade (with the obscenities excised here), she roars, "I shoulda aborted your ass! . . . I knew it when the doctor put you in my goddam hand you wasn't a goddam thing! You wear that smirk on your face, bitch?" She heaves a glass that lands at her daughter's feet. "Now smile about that, you fat bitch!"

Venturing inside Mary Johnston's mind, one finds a disturbed but poignant rationalization for her misbehavior. "Real women *sacrifice*!" she tells Precious. And Mary sacrificed Precious: she allowed her to be raped by her father so that he would continue to have sex with her. To the social worker Mrs. Weiss (Mariah Carey), Mary cries, "Who else was going to love me? Who else was going to touch me?

Who else was going to make me feel good about myself?" In scenes like this one, audiences must bow, or cringe, before the explosion of malice, cunning and finally self-pity that Mo'Nique displays as Precious's brutal mom. A stand-up comedian by trade, Mo'Nique commands the screen even in those infrequent moments when her character's not doing something awful. She does more than bring what could be a cartoon of malice to vivid screen life; she makes a dreadful emotional sense of the Worst Mom Ever.

. . . AND *NOW, VOYAGER*

We can't leave it at this. Too many exposed nerves, too much genetic detritus in these stories of women whose motherly legacy is the pain of their children. Old movies aren't the only form of entertainment that requires a happy ending. Some book chapters do as well. So let us return to our first bad-mothers example and see if Charlotte Vale managed to crawl from under the rock of her mother's evil and find the sunlight. At night.

Charlotte, the heiress, has checked herself back into Dr. Jaquith's spa-clinic, where she meets Tina (Janis Wilson), the troubled twelve-year-old daughter of Charlotte's erstwhile lover Jerry. Fleeing from conflicts with her own mother, Tina is a next-generation image of Charlotte's dismal life before Jerry. Charlotte takes the girl out for ice cream and camping trips and at night comforts the crying Tina. "This is Jerry's child in my arms," she says in ecstatic voice-over. "This is Jerry's child clinging to me." Propriety, and Dr. Jaquith's strict instructions, may keep Charlotte from resuming her affair with an unhappily married man. But she can be his daughter's mother, in a way, by bringing the child to live with her in the Vale mansion. Jerry gets visitation rights, and Charlotte says, "We can talk about your child." "Our child," he says, correcting her. Their love is expressed through joint custody of Tina and by sharing the cigarettes he lights, two at a time. "Oh, Jerry, don't let's ask for the moon," says the woman who has freed herself from the grasp of a bad mother by becoming a wonderful one. "We have the stars."

White Heat, 1949: James Cagney as Cody Jarrett and Margaret Wycherly
as the mother who spurred him to the top of the world.

CRIME AND HORROR MOMS

Whether breaking the law or battling demons, they never forget their kids.

"Don't know what I'd do without ya, Ma," the gangster Cody Jarrett (James Cagney) tells his enabling mom as he sits on her lap and she pours him a shot of whiskey. "Well," Norman Bates (Anthony Perkins) primly observes, "a boy's best friend is his mother." In two violent genres—crime movies like *White Heat* and the horror films inspired by *Psycho*—a mother would seize center screen by working her will on her offspring. That influence was often malignant, occasionally benign.

157

But both varieties tended to illustrate the ferocious devotion of a mother to her child. They also gave actresses the opportunity to embody women who *did things*, heroic or egregious, rather than simply stand by and watch men escalate the body count.

CRIME MOMS

In *The Public Enemy*, the 1931 gangster film that made him a star, Cagney played Tom Powers, a tough guy with a naïve, doting mother and an abusive father, a cop, who dealt out punishment with a leather strop. (At the end, Tom's enemies deliver his body, wrapped like a parcel, to his mother's doorstep, as she fluffs his bedroom pillows, awaiting her prodigal son's return.) Cagney felt straitjacketed by hoodlum roles and played none in the decade after 1939's *The Roaring Twenties*. But when he revisited the genre to play Cody, the career criminal in director Raoul Walsh's 1949 classic **White Heat**, Cagney lent full force to his portrait of a sociopath with an Oedipus complex.

Ma Jarrett (Margaret Wycherly, who was Gary Cooper's mother in *Sergeant York*) pours all her ardor and craftiness into Cody; she massages his roiling skull, offers canny advice on eluding the Feds, runs the gang when he's in prison and goes out to buy his favorite strawberries—inadvertently tipping off the law to the gang's hideout. Cody treats her as mother and spouse, and ignores his slatternly wife, Verna (Virginia Mayo), as if she were a tropical disease. Verna responds by betraying Cody, as any woman but his mother would. Cody recognizes that Ma was also bred to a life of crime. "Some life!" he sneers. "First there was my old man, died kickin' and screamin' in a nuthouse. Then my brother. And after that, it was takin' care of me. Always tryin' to put me on top. 'Top of the world,' she used to say." At the end, cornered atop a huge gas-storage tank, he pumps bullets into the facility and shouts, "Made it, Ma! Top of the world!" *Boooom!* Now he can join her.

This primal modern crime movie—written by Ivan Goff and Ben Roberts, who later created the pinup-detective TV series *Charlie's Angels*—establishes a Freudian basis for Cody's behavior, exactly as Alfred Hitchcock's *Psycho*, the primal modern horror film, would do for Norman Bates eleven years later. "The only person he's ever cared about or trusted is his mother," a Treasury Department man (John Archer) tells Hank Fallon (Edmond O'Brien), the undercover agent assigned to infiltrate Cody's gang. "No one else has ever made a dent, not even his wife. His mother's been the prop that's held him up. He's got a fierce, psychopathic devotion for her. All his life, whenever he got in a spot, he just put out his hand and there was Ma Jarrett." Fallon's job is to worm his way into Cody's trust and "take Mama's place. . . . I'll practice up on my lullabies." In another *Psycho* premonition, the shot of Cody's face dissolving into his mother's anticipates the climactic dissolve of Norman's face into his mother's skull. And after Ma's death, Cody has a Norman-like conversation with her ghost. "That was a good feelin' out there," he says, "talkin' to her, just me and Ma. Good feelin'. Liked it." He pauses to reflect: "Maybe I *am* nuts."

Criminals of a more ambitious sort—Nazis in South America, just after the war, with a uranium cache—tiptoe Teutonically through *Notorious* (1946), the Hitchcock thriller famous for a wine bottle filled with uranium dust and the record-length kissing scene between Cary Grant and Ingrid Bergman. Grant, as U.S. secret agent Devlin, must convince Bergman's Alicia Huberman, the promiscuous daughter of a Nazi bigwig, to fly down to Rio and cozy up to another Nazi, Alexander Sebastian (Claude Rains). Her undercover assignment extends to marrying Sebastian, who has fallen in love with her, while taking orders from Devlin, who insults and mistreats Alicia and puts her life in jeopardy; he loves her too, but duty comes first. Indeed, the Nazi, not the Fed, is the only male character with a purchase on audience sympathy: whatever his war crimes, Sebastian is the smitten dupe. The only member of his entourage who sees through Alicia's scheme is his mother (Leopoldine Konstantin, billed as Madame Konstantin). Like Ma Jarrett, the sepulchral Frau Sebastian can smell betrayal in her son's wife.

Hitchcock cleverly cast Rains, fifty-six when the movie was shot, as a paternal figure to Bergman, then thirty—a suaver, more affectionate version of Alicia's own father. Konstantin, just three years older than Rains, serves as Sebastian's grasping mother and early warning system for all suspicious outsiders. His sharp instincts occluded by love, he attributes her misgivings to spite: "You've always been jealous of any woman I've shown any interest in." When he discovers the wine bottle Devlin has tampered with, and realizes that Alicia gave Devlin the keys to the cellar, the little man sinks into a cuckolded husband's despair and goes to the only person who might save him. When he begs his mother for help, she tartly replies, "We are protected by the enormity of your stupidity." Their wills now merged in his peril, they begin poisoning Alicia. As the drug takes effect and her senses blur, she sees two figures fuse into a single image: mother and son, Rio's first family of the Third Reich.

Arizona "Arrie" Clark, known to the law and the tabloid press as Kate "Ma" Barker, cared for her kids, at least as played by Shelley Winters in Roger Corman's 1970 film **Bloody Mama**. The real Ma Barker may have been only an accomplice to the crimes of her four sons, but the script, by Robert Thom and Don Peters, promotes her to mastermind. The 1967 *Bonnie and Clyde* cued a spate of biopics on the most wanted criminals of the 1930s. Using the same mixture of bloodshed and broad comedy, the Corman film had its own theme song: "Ma Barker taught her boys / To play with guns like toys . . ."

Bloody Mama, like *White Heat* before it, provides a psychological backstory to explain its protagonist's errant ways: As a girl, Kate was brutalized by her father and brothers. Turning an excess of abuse into an excess of love, Kate dominates her grown sons, Herman (Don Stroud), Arthur (Clint Kimbrough), Fred (Robert Walden) and Lloyd (the young Robert De Niro). What might be tender affection from another mother—washing Herman's back and chest as he takes a bath, flirting with Lloyd to get him to sample her homemade cookies, leading the lads in a group sing of the antiwar anthem "I Didn't Raise My Boy to Be a Soldier"—is for Ma the hothouse flowering of derangement. She raised her boys to rob banks and shoot cops, and when the sons develop a fondness for a businessman (Pat Hingle) they have kidnapped, Ma recognizes the threat of an appealing father figure and orders them to kill him. (They don't.) The sons may be Cody Jarrett quadrupled—four kinds of poisonous nuts—but Ma, as Winters plays her, is a villain of grandeur. The actress shoots out so much demonic energy that the machine gun she carries is a redundant appliance.

leek and sinewy where Winters was buxom, Angie Dickinson played the fictional Wilma McClatchie in another Depression-era drama, ***Big Bad Mama*** (1974), produced by Corman and directed by Steve Carver from a script by William W. Norton and Frances Doel. Instead of four grown sons, Wilma has two teenage daughters, blond Billy Jean (Susan Sennett) and brunette Polly (Robbie Lee), both as man-hungry as Mom. While dispensing maternal *mots*—"Keep your

Bloody Mama, 1970: Shelley Winters as Ma Barker; one of her sons was the young Robert De Niro.

legs together, Billie Jean, and shut up"—Wilma also runs their lives in a fashion that merges the protective with the exploitative. She bursts into a men's-club smoker and wrests her girls from the shame of stripping, which they were eager to do. "A mother's still got rights in this country," Wilma announces as she fleeces the club of its treasury. With the FBI in pursuit, she takes over a bootlegging operation and falls in with a bank robber (Tom Skerritt) and a gambler (William Shatner), whose favors she occasionally shares with her randy kids.

Like a Dust Bowl Scarlett O'Hara, Wilma keeps saying, "We ain't ever gonna be poor again." These are her dying words—though Dickinson miraculously reappeared, thirteen years later, in the Corman-produced *Big Bad Mama II*, where a slightly more righteous Wilma indulges in criminal behavior to expose the venality of the land baron who foreclosed on her house. As she tells one of her kids: "Your mama may not always be right, but Mama will always be Mama." Well, she's right about that.

They don't call firebugs "arson auteurs" or serial stabbers "knife surgeons." Yet the underworldlings who separate marks from their money are known as con artists, perhaps because the tools of their trade are the gifts of a great actor's performance: glamour, intimacy, cool patter, the steady stare that conceals the lie. Doesn't a mother rely on similar subterfuges to get her child to eat his kale or stop crying? Con artists might deserve the name "gifters," but Jim Thompson labeled them *The Grifters* in his 1963 paperback original about three dissemblers who play their deadliest tricks on one another. It's only fitting that, in the book and the 1990 film adaptation written by Donald E. Westlake and directed by Stephen Frears, two of these should be mother and son.

Roy Dillon (John Cusack) works the "short con," using loaded dice and legerdemain to skin cashiers and sailors. Roy's girlfriend Myra (Annette Bening) is cheaper and perkier, aiming for the "long con"—the elaborate scheme that takes suckers for big stakes. And Roy's mother Lilly (Anjelica Huston) is the con woman supreme. Abused and abusing since girlhood, she can pull off a motel-room kill and do it with a hard smirk. She can also stand up for Roy, at least when he's been seriously wounded by a baseball bat after a grift went wrong. "My son is going to be all

Big Bad Mama, 1974: Angie Dickinson with her daughters, Susan Sennett and Robbie Lee, and their escorts, William Shatner and Tom Skerritt.

right," she tells the hospital doctor. "If not, I'll have you killed." Lilly means she'll call on the muscle of her bookmaker boss Bobo Justus (Pat Hingle, having survived *Bloody Mama*), a sadist who imposes discipline by burning Lilly's hand with a lighted cigar when she ducks out on a job. She explains she did it to tend to Roy, and Bobo, nonplussed, asks, "What the f— are you doing with a son?"

Roy must wonder that too. He is grateful for Lilly's fast work in the hospital. "I guess I owe you my life, Lilly," he says, and she, imposing the bond of motherhood, replies, "You always did, Roy." But this typical Thompson antihero—a smart guy getting outsmarted by fate, fast company or himself—doesn't stand much of a chance with a mother who is barely fifteen years older than he is and who treats him, in her friendlier moments, less as a boy than as a beau. He can rebuff her seductions, but he can't duck her wrath. Neither can Myra, who's also a bit older than Roy and plies her sexuality to pay the rent or pawn a jewel. They might be battling mother figures at war over custody of Roy's sooty soul. Huston (in a role once meant for Cher) and Bening make for two splendidly sexy carnivores, with Cusack as the would-be lion tamer whose destiny is to be devoured. Guess who finally dines on Roy? The one crime-movie mother who isn't ready to die for her son but can find a reason to kill him.

Not every crime mother is hard as nails. One is as soft as Charmin tissue, until she's pushed to extremes because the lurid mores of modern America are not the ones she has tried to instill in her children. In **Serial Mom**, Beverly Sutphin (Kathleen Turner) is a suburban matron with a caring dentist husband, Eugene (Sam Waterston), and two fairly normal teenage kids named Misty (Ricki Lake) and Chip (Matthew Lillard). She also has an urge to kill anyone who affronts her antique notion of decency. If someone should chastise her children or date a fast girl or wear white after Labor Day, Mom goes maniacal.

You could say that the fifties made her do it. Anyway, fifties family sitcoms. Forty years later, Beverly wants to live—does live, poor deranged dear—in the white-bread, Populuxe world of Ozzie and Harriet Nelson. Modern movies? "They're so violent." When Chip lets slip the word "shit," Mother reproves him: "You know how I hate

The Grifters, 1990: Mother Anjelica Huston and girlfriend Annette Bening
contend over which one of them gets to destroy John Cusack.

the brown word." As her crimes escalate, and with them her tabloid renown, Chip gently asks his mother if she's a serial killer. Beverly responds, with an indulgent smile, "The only serial I know anything about is Rice Krispies." But the cops don't buy her pristine propriety. "All units," the radio bulletin sounds. "Serial Mom is headed south on Keswick. Proceed with caution. She is armed and f———in' nuts."

Should we have mentioned earlier that John Waters's movie is a comedy? And not so much about a compulsive murderer as about the modern mix of celebrity and notoriety? (Patty Hearst played the juror who gets whacked for wearing white.) "My movies aren't about violence," Waters has said, "but about how America is so confused about fame." *Serial Mom*, which came out a few months before the O. J. Simpson killings and trial, offers further evidence that in the modern United States, the wages of sin are stardom. Beverly has earned role-model rep when a friend of Misty's asks, "Can I borrow your mother? My aunt is coming for dinner, and she's always getting on my nerves." In Waters's world, even a killer's family stays true to her. "Is it menopausal?" asks a worried but sympathetic Eugene, who tells the kids, "No matter what your mother is, we'll love her anyway."

Janine "Smurf" Cody (Jacki Weaver) seems every inch the sassy Aussie mom, brandishing a steely-cheery attitude gleaned from some *Carry On* film or *Benny Hill* sketch. But in writer-director David Michôd's 2010 film ***Animal Kingdom***, Smurf is the leader of a Melbourne crime family. Family, literally, for the gang comprises Smurf's three sons: Andrew (Ben Mendelsohn), whom everyone, from reverence or fear, calls Pope; Craig (Sullivan Stapleton), a hyperactive coke addict who sells drugs; and Darren (Luke Ford), the youngest, who tags along on his brothers' sprees. They are joined by their seventeen-year-old nephew J (James Frecheville) after his mother dies of a heroin overdose. Turns out she was the renegade white sheep of the family, keeping J away from her toxic clan—and especially from the smiling Smurf, who sees every malicious act as a moral imperative. Her own eleventh commandment: "We do what we have to do, we do what we must. Just because we don't want to do something doesn't mean it can't be done."

Based loosely on the 1980s exploits of Kath Pettingill, whose sons were convicted

Serial Mom, 1994: Beverly Sutphin (Kathleen Turner) has a loving husband (Sam Waterston), two nice teen kids (Ricki Lake and Matthew Lillard) and an urge to kill the people whose lifestyles she disapproves of.

of armed robbery and acquitted of murder, *Animal Kingdom* also implicitly cites *White Heat*: Cody Jarrett, meet Janine Cody. Smurf's sons are just as dependent on her as Cody was on Ma. More than a comforter and abettor to her sons' misbehavior, she is their spiritual guide—the petite, purring, bleach-blond fountainhead of the family disease. A twisted parody of maternal devotion, Smurf gives a full-mouth kiss to one son, snuggles on the lap of another, counsels that "it's all right to cry" when hearing bad news and suggests that Pope might want to go back on his meds. When she learns that J could be persuaded by a Melbourne detective (Guy Pearce) to give state's evidence against his uncles, Smurf pinwheels into action, hatching a plot to get rid of a bad seed who might turn good. Weaver earned an Oscar nomination for playing this pert agent of iniquity. Hers is an ordinary suburban, dead-thrilling kind of evil. She makes the best bad mama of twenty-first-century crime movies.

Honorable mention in this category goes to Kristin Scott Thomas, that aristocratic icon of English and French cinema, who has wicked fun as Crystal in Nicolas Winding Refn's 2013 film ***Only God Forgives***. Spitting obscenities at the world, depraved by greed and mother love, Crystal runs a drug-smuggling syndicate; her elder son, Julian (Ryan Gosling), manages the Bangkok branch. She flies in from the States on learning of the death of her younger son, Billy (Tom Burke). Told that Billy raped and slaughtered a sixteen-year-old girl, Crystal shrugs: "I'm sure he had his reasons." No wonder both her sons are Oedipal wrecks.

Some crime-family movie mothers—like Morgana King as Mama Corleone in the first two *Godfather* films—knew their place: in the kitchen, away from the dirty business. Profiting from the blood money that sustained their family, they could pretend that hubby made his stash in the olive oil business they took no part in. Others, like Ma Jarrett, Ma Barker, Wilma McClatchie and Smurf Cody, ran the family crime business with the ruthless brio of working-class women elbowing into a men-only job. Scott Thomas's Crystal, dolled up in a blond hairdo and slinky clothes, represents the next generation, the new breed of crime mother: a career woman who chose to make her millions through drug smuggling instead of, say, investment banking.

One thing never changed, though. Crystal, Mrs. Sebastian, the Mas Jarrett and Barker, Wilma McClatchie and Smurf Cody—they did it for their kids. Beverly Sutphin did it in a desperate rear-guard belief that her children should grow up in the same antiseptic environment she did. Only *The Grifters'* Lilly stands outside this group. Not protective but predatory, she consumes her young for the same reason a mama scorpion does: she's still hungry.

HORROR MOMS

Sometimes, not seeing is believing. In Alfred Hitchcock's **Psycho** (1960), Norman Bates's mother is a spectral presence: glimpsed behind a window shade or a shower curtain, heard chastising her son ("Huh, boy? You have the guts, boy?"), or viewed indistinctly from above, carried by Norman from her bedroom to the fruit cellar. Only at the end do we get a quick hard look at Mrs. Bates: a mummified corpse, her hollow eyes seeming to move as a light swings above her. But she has dominated the film, because of the postmortem influence she holds on her son. Norma Bates lives in Norman (Anthony Perkins); her fury stoked his madness. "He tried to be his mother," says the psychiatrist (Simon Oakland) at the end of the movie. "And now he is."

Psycho, scripted by Joseph Stefano from Robert Bloch's novel, set new rules for the horror genre. Rather, it said the old rules no longer applied. A movie could kill off the major character in the second act; it could turn a nice guy into a psychopath who is also a victim; it could be both clinically realistic and artistically adventurous in the depiction of violence. The first major slasher movie, *Psycho* established the incestuous connection of prurience and puritanism: show a pretty woman undressed, then punish her display, and the viewer's voyeurism, in the shower. Virtually all modern horror films flow from this exalted source.

Modern horror, like ancient Greek tragedy from Jocasta and Oedipus to Medea and her unlucky offspring, often resides in the relationship between mother and son. *Psycho* came out at the popular crest of Freudian psychoanalysis, which traced an adult's emotional wounds to an infantile trauma involving the mother. In the 2012 film *Hitchcock*, a fictional retelling of the making of *Psycho*, Stefano (Ralph Macchio)

Psycho, 1960: "A boy's best friend is his mother."

tells Hitch (Anthony Hopkins) that he spends a lot of time in therapy talking to his shrink about "the usual things: sex, rage, my mother . . ." Click. Whether or not that conversation took place, Stefano and, no less, Perkins crept inside Norman to provide a superb study of derangement, of a dual, dueling personality, of a grown child strangled by his umbilical tether to his mother—a theme of which succeeding horror films would take extensive note.

To Marion Crane (Janet Leigh), his guest for the evening at the Bates Motel, Norman can perceptively and charmingly discuss his widowed mother's failings and his loyalty to her: "If you love somebody, you wouldn't leave them even if they treat you badly. Do you understand? I don't hate my mother. I hate what she's become. I hate her illness." When Marion suggests putting Mrs. Bates "someplace," meaning an asylum, Norman lashes out: "Have you ever seen the inside of one of those places? The laughing, and the tears, and those cruel eyes studying you?" (Apparently he has.) He sees his mother's disease as a facet of her quirky humanity: "It's not like my mother is a maniac or a raving thing. She just goes a little mad sometimes. We all go a little mad sometimes," he says, and asks his visitor, "Haven't you?"

Norman went a little—a lot—mad long ago, when he killed his mother after she told him she was marrying another man, effectively ending her exclusive relationship with her son. (He also murdered the interloping man—a casual casualty of his envious wrath.) Now, briefly, he has connected with Marion, who, on the run after stealing $40,000 from her boss, privately resolves to return home. She won't get there because, having shared a sandwich and a soulful chat with Norman, she just graduated to number one on Mother Bates's to-kill list. (She is collateral damage of the jealous-mother side of Norman.) But this man still loved the thing he killed. To keep Mother near, he husbanded her corpse and taxidermized it, wore her dress, spoke in her voice and, when Marion took a shower, became his vengeful mom. The psychiatrist: "He was never all Norman, but he was often only Mother."

Psycho eventually devolved into a franchise: three sequels, all starring Perkins, then Gus Van Sant's shot-by-shot 1998 remake with Vince Vaughn, and now an A&E series, *Bates Motel*. In this origins story, which imagines how mother and son constructed the cage they can never crawl out of, Norma (Vera Farmiga) fiercely shelters and dotes on the seventeen-year-old Norman (Freddie Highmore), doing her best to annihilate all pretty girls who might distract him from her love. The Hitchcock film, until its last scene, explains little about Mrs. Bates and shows less. The Master of Suspense would never tip his hand about a movie mystery. But the audience learned all it needed to know about Mother from her nagging and knifing, and from the fear, love and madness in Norman's eyes.

A mean mother and the weak son who takes postmortem power from her: that was *Psycho*. All the crimes could be attributed to natural, if creepy and twisted, motives. But in the Vietnam years—when, not to overstate the case, *everything* in popular culture changed—upscale horror films found a new explanation for a son's or daughter's infernal streak. The root of all evil shifted from the natural to the supernatural, from the secular to the religious. Could it be . . . Satan?

"What Jesus was to the 1950s movie epic," wrote Roger Ebert in his review of *The Omen*, "the devil is to the 1970s." In that film and two important predecessors, a child from hell had a decent earthly mother. Lucifer, or rather his near relation the antichrist, was the force behind 1968's **Rosemary's Baby**, filmed by Roman Polanski

Rosemary's Baby, 1968: Mia Farrow, impregnated by the devil, ponders weighty issues.

from Ira Levin's bestseller. Frustrated actor Guy (John Cassavetes) makes a deal with the devil: get me the starring role in a play and you can have Satan impregnate my wife, Rosemary (Mia Farrow). By the merest chance, some of Guy's neighbors in their new Central Park West apartment house are members of a coven who drug Rosemary on the night the Horned One will debauch her. She had planned dreamily for her first child, but not This One. At the culmination of her arduous pregnancy, when Rosemary first sees her demon baby, a small smile wreathes her face, as if she believes that a good mother can handle a difficult child. Adrian may be Satan's son, but he will always be Rosemary's baby.

Pregnancy and delivery are just the first two traumas mothers endure. A dozen or so years after, they must monitor the child's volcanic changes of body and mood, otherwise known as puberty. In the 1973 film ***The Exorcist***, directed by William Friedkin from William Peter Blatty's novel and screenplay, single mom Chris MacNeil (Ellen Burstyn) notices that her daughter Regan (Linda Blair) is suffering from even more troubling symptoms: she spits out obscenities, causes her bed to shake and has traded in Captain Howdy, her imaginary friend from childhood, for a demon named Pazuzu. Chris can't be the first fretful mother to say of her twelve-year-old, "That *thing* upstairs isn't my daughter." Regan's, though, is a rarer case: not of rambunctious hormones but of satanic possession. The agnostic mom must brush away sensible skepticism and employ two Catholic priests (Jason Miller and Max von Sydow) who specialize in exorcism.

The first horror movie to be nominated for the Best Picture Oscar, with Burstyn, Miller and Blair nominees in the acting categories, *The Exorcist* was a popular smash—ninth on the all-time list of real-dollar box-office grossers. The movie earned its notoriety from its high fright quotient and from the obscenities that the demon expels through Regan (euphemized in the first season of *Saturday Night Live* as "Your mama sews socks that smell!"). But at its tremulous heart, this is a love story about a mother who will try anything, beyond science or sense, to rid her child of the attitudes, the disease, the demons that have seized her.

Lee Remick, that glistening American beauty, and movie patriarch Gregory Peck: how could they be the parents of the antichrist? Through some strenuous plot exertions by David Seltzer in his original screenplay for the 1976 film ***The Omen***. Katherine Thorn (Remick) gives birth in Rome to a son who soon dies. To secure her emotional stability, Katherine's wealthy diplomat husband Robert (Peck) follows the suggestion of a local priest and adopts the child of a woman who gave birth that same night. Bad idea for Robert, smart for the movie, since the boy, Damien (Harvey Spencer Stephens), is the Book of Revelation's jackal-born antichrist, complete with a retinue of enabling, infernal nannies. One of these handmaidens hangs herself from the Thorn roof; another, Mrs. Baylock (Billie Whitelaw), shows up to comfort the parents and raise the little one to his prophesized stature: "Have no fear, little one. I am here to protect Thee."

The Exorcist, 1973: Ellen Burstyn tries to soothe her sweet, Satan-possessed daughter, Linda Blair.

And Damien is there to rid the world of Robert and Katherine—his first step to ascending the apocalyptic throne. He bangs his tricycle against a stepladder Katherine is perched on, causing her to miscarry the child who might have been a nuisance or a rival. As Katherine recuperates, she is pushed out of a high window by Mrs. Baylock, who must think of herself as the true mother Damien never had. And when Robert resolves to kill his adopted son, the son wins. The surprise of director Richard Donner's stolid, solid film was the demise of the parents who served as audience surrogates. That innovation proved a prophecy: from then on, stars would be less important than franchises. With *The Omen* on its way to becoming a trilogy, Peck and Remick, and William Holden and Lee Grant in 1978's *Damien: Omen II*, were disposable commodities, as was the time-honored notion of heroic mothers who went through hell to nurture a better world. In sequels, only the antichild need survive.

Stephen King is the Oliver Sacks of horror fiction. As Sacks has documented unusual cases of people with neurological disorders that can seem like gifts, so King creates ordinary people blessed or cursed with extraordinary abilities: the girl with pyrokinetic powers in *Firestarter*, the death-row inmate with the gift of healing in *The Green Mile*. In his first published novel he related the story of a teen girl's telekinesis, triggered like a mega-explosion of puberty in the high school shower. The book already bore kid-sister similarities to Norman Bates and *Psycho*. And when Brian De Palma, Hitchcock's most persistent imitator, directed the 1976 movie of **Carrie**, he underlined the connection by changing the girl's Thomas Ewen Consolidated School to . . . Bates High School.

Poor Carrie (Sissy Spacek) suffers vicious taunting from her classmates, but her first and final torturer is her mother, Margaret (Piper Laurie), an evangelical kook as virulent as Mrs. Bates. Foregrounding the mother-daughter antagonism, and pushing their final confrontation to the film's climax, De Palma and screenwriter Lawrence D. Cohen fashioned the most vivid specimens of a possessive parent with murderous intent and a meek child driven to revenge.

Carrie has always been a reproach to her mother: Margaret's late husband, with whom she had "lived sinlessly," got drunk one night and had sex with her, and, even worse, Margaret says, "I liked it!" Carrie's existence is a constant reminder of that moral crime to a woman who believes that religion is "spreading the gospel of God's salvation through Christ's blood" but that "the Lord visited Eve with the curse, and the curse was the curse of blood." Carrie's first menstrual period (which Margaret never prepared her for) marks the visitation of that curse on the next generation. Margaret regrets having brought Carrie into the world and, at the end, tries to take her out of it, which triggers the girl's last violent eruption of telekinesis. Yet Carrie feels a tenderness for her mother; her final impulse is to save her. This important gesture is missing in the inferior 2013 remake starring Chloë Grace Moretz and Julianne Moore, where horror-film vengeance overcomes the love for a deranged mother.

·   ·   ·

Carrie, 1976: Blaming her daughter, Carrie (Sissy Spacek), for all sins of the flesh, Margaret White (Piper Laurie) prepares to exact some Old Testament retribution.

Mothers may lurch into madness from hating their children or from loving and losing them. In Wes Craven's ***The Last House on the Left*** (1972), a kind of slasher remake of Ingmar Bergman's *The Virgin Spring*, a husband and wife, upon learning that the four strangers staying the night have slaughtered their daughter, determine to take grisly revenge. Sean S. Cunningham, the producer of *Last House*, then borrowed from *Psycho* for his *Friday the 13th* franchise. Jason Voorhees, the hockey-masked angel of death, was not the killer of the Crystal Lake camp counselors in the original 1980 *Friday* film. His mother, Pamela (Betsy Palmer), had blamed the camp for the death by drowning of her teenage son twenty-three years before and came back to massacre the next generation of counselors. In the sequels, Jason, revived by the miraculous science of Hollywood greed, did his own dirty work. But the 2009 reboot begins with the boy witnessing his mother's beheading after her murder spree. Decades later, Jason (Derek Mears) returns to kidnap a girl, Whitney (Amanda Righetti), who looks just like Pamela—as if Norman Bates had found a living replica of Norma. Whitney, no fool, pretends to be Pamela, distracting the smitten Jason long enough to eviscerate him with his own machete. Son and "mother" lock one last time in intimate enmity.

At the heart of these films is a parent's grief at the loss of a child. The old are meant to die, the young to live. A child's death upends and outrages that natural order, leaving its gravest mark on the woman who bore and raised the child. A mature mother is expected to deal with it, tend the emotional wound until, with time, scar tissue forms. She may even take pride in her children's sacrifice, as Alleta Sullivan (Selena Royle) did in *The Fighting Sullivans* (1944), after all five of her sons were killed together at Guadalcanal. But an unstable mother may never recover from the signal atrocity of her child's death and may choose a more drastic remedy: evening the score through the catharsis of violence. If she did not love and grieve so fiercely, she would not act so furiously. Such a mother is the patron demon of horror films—though they usually spend less time probing the inconsolable ache than reveling in the repellent spectacle. Melodrama reduces sad moms to mad moms, and over the movie decades their march has grown to parade proportions.

Two of the most popular, profitable movies of 2013 unleashed the ancient spirits of killer moms to haunt modern families, and in each film, an outside mother figure intervenes, confronting evil with her own surprising strength. In Andrés Muschietti's richly atmospheric *Mama*, Annabel (Jessica Chastain) realizes that a maleficent force has claimed the two young nieces of her boyfriend. The ghost, whom the girls call Mama, was a nineteenth-century woman, Edith Brennan, sent to an insane asylum, her only child given to nuns. She escaped the asylum, retrieved her baby and, pursued by the law, jumped off a cliff to her death. Not realizing her infant was snagged on a tree branch and saved, Edith has taken Annabel's nieces as living avatars of the child she thought dead. Annabel must summon her own protective maternal instincts to try prying the girls from Mama's clutches.

The malignant force in director James Wan's *The Conjuring* is another nineteenth-century spirit: the witch Bathsheba, who slaughtered her children and, before killing herself, laid a curse on anyone who would occupy her Rhode Island home. In the 1970s, when the Perrons, Carolyn (Lili Taylor) and Roger (Ron Livingston), unwittingly move in with their five daughters, they sense Bathsheba's wrath and call on two real-life ghostbusters, Lorraine (Vera Farmiga) and Ed Warren (Patrick Wilson), famed for their exorcism of a Long Island house that inspired the 1979 film *The Amityville Horror*. Bathsheba soon co-opts Carolyn's will, forcing her to attempt killing her daughters, and Lorraine must find a way around the witch to reach the good mother she hopes Carolyn still is.

A huge critical and popular hit, *The Conjuring* plays it straight. Like *Mama*, it abjures CGI gimmicks and instead weaves an ominous mood out of long takes, astute performances from splendid actors—especially Farmiga, taking a break from Norma Bates to play a mother figure who is savior, not corrupter—and that most terrifying of aural effects: silence. Both *Mama* and *The Conjuring* ignore the more lurid *Psycho* imitations of the past half century and return to the pristine Hitchcock model: dramatizing the spell that the dead cast on the living, and a clinging mother on the children she left behind.

On Being a Mother and Actress

"Ahhh . . . a daughter of great fortune!" said the mysterious tea leaf reader at the Russian Tea Room in New York City as she looked into my eyes. I will never forget that statement, made several years prior to the birth of my beautiful daughter, Melanie Griffith, at Doctors Hospital in New York.

When Melanie was put into my arms, I told her she was beautiful and that she was going to have a very special life. That phrase from the tea leaf reader has often proven to be true. Even as a child, Melanie was giving, thoughtful, funny, sensitive—loved animals and was always so kind and loving to them. She began displaying her independence and self-assuredness around age one, liked to mimic me and was always interested in what I was doing. She loved books; she still does. We loved shopping; we still do. She loved playing with makeup; we still do.

Her father, the late Peter Griffith, and I divorced when she was two years old. I was a working mom—as a fashion model with the Eileen Ford Agency, later doing TV commercials, the residuals from which made our lives financially secure. It was difficult at times, but we learned to make it work. Melanie's nanny, the late Josephine Milton, was a good teacher to Melanie and they liked each other, which made it much easier for me as I would so have loved to be with Melanie all the time. All of those feelings strongly made decisions for me. By the time Melanie was four, I felt we should have a house where she could just say, "Mommy, I'm going out to play," which wasn't possible living in a New York City apartment. So all of us packed up—Melanie, me, Josephine, the puppy, the kitty—and off we flew to Los Angeles, where I rented a wonderful home in Westwood.

I thought my career as a fashion model and in commercials would go on as it had in New York. But it didn't. I was worried. Then, on Friday the thirteenth of October, 1961, along came the call from an executive at Universal Studios asking if I was the woman in the Sego Pet Milk commercial. I was. A few days later I was under contract to Alfred Hitchcock, though he had seen only my reel of about fifteen commercials and my book of fashion photos. I was asked by the agent at MCA to read the contract carefully, and, if I approved of it, to sign it, and we would then go to the studio to meet Mr. Hitchcock! I could hardly wait to get home and tell Melanie we were going to be all right. Our lives had changed.

At the time, children weren't as welcome on film sets as they are today, but Melanie was allowed to be on the set of *The Birds* (1963) to meet Mr. Hitchcock, Rod Taylor, Suzanne Pleshette and Jessica Tandy. Then came *Marnie* (1964), another Hitchcock film, so Melanie met Sean Connery, Diane Baker and Louise Latham.

My real-life role as Melanie's mom had made me more aware of the complexities of Marnie and the complicated life she had experienced. All life situations come to aid you in the roles you play.

It was all very exciting, on the surface. I never talked to anyone but my sister Patty about the difficult situation I was having at the studio. By the end of *Marnie* I ended the relationship with Hitchcock. I demanded to be let out of my contract, but he refused to let that happen. He said he would ruin my career, and he did. He continued to pay me for almost two years, turning down roles offered to me, saying, "She isn't available."

Luckily, I received a call from Charlie Chaplin to join Marlon Brando, Sophia Loren and Charlie's son Sydney in *A Countess from Hong Kong* (1967). So off we went to London. Melanie had a really wonderful time with Sophia. That amazing lady took Melanie under her wing and they were inseparable. I could see Sophia would make a really caring, devoted mother, and later she did. We love Sophia.

As a mother, I probably should have suspected that all of these experiences would encourage Melanie to become an actress. As years went by, she became more beautiful by the minute. Soon she was cast in big films, one after the other. The most important in my eyes was *Working Girl* (1988), for which she earned an Academy Award nomination for Best Actress. I believe Melanie's role as a real-life mother gave her so many acting tools to excel in scenes with children, as is clear in her films *Milk Money* (1994) and *Crazy in Alabama* (1999), featuring her real-life children. Melanie is the most creative woman I have ever known, and I am so proud of her for her honesty, her bravery and her capacity to love. She is also the best mother to my three beautiful grandchildren!

Bless my "daughter of great fortune"! I love her more than my next breath. And a great tip of my hat to that mystical tea leaf reader. She had it so right!

—Tippi Hedren

Close Encounters of the Third Kind, 1977: Melinda Dillon and her four-year-old son (Cary Guffey) who talks to aliens.

SCI-FI MOMS

They face down aliens, benign or devouring, to protect their kids.

"Oh, come on," says Sarah Connor, a lonely L.A. waitress who's just been told she is destined to give birth to a child who will save the world. "Do I look like the mother of the future?" She does if she is the heroine of a science-fiction film, a genre that turns the impossible into the plausible. Sci-fi typically launches muscular guys on a mission to conquer the solar system through superior weaponry and battle skills. But in some of the finest examples, the hero is a woman: a mother-to-be like

Sarah in *The Terminator*, a single mom in *Close Encounters of the Third Kind*, a woman warrior who discovers the mother within her when she defends an orphan girl in *Aliens*. In the Superman reboot *Man of Steel*, she is the caring adoptive mom who instills the finest American values in an alien boy named Clark Kent.

In several of the films, humanity makes contact with the metaphorical divine; science-fiction writers are as fond of Jesus analogies as horror writers are of Satan figures. But all of these mothers show how caring for children can contribute to saving the planet.

Two events in the late 1940s cued science fiction's graduation from the pulp magazines to the movie screen: the onset of the Cold War, in which the U.S. and the USSR became global rivals armed with atomic and hydrogen bombs, and the spreading stories of unidentified flying objects—flying saucers—in America's skies. If we weren't going to die in a nuclear Armageddon, or if our small towns and coastal cities didn't face destruction by insects or lizards that A-bomb fallout had irradiated into giant monsters, then we might be invaded or annihilated by evil spacemen! Dozens of no-budget movies throughout the fifties energetically exploited this nexus of popular fear. But among the earliest A-budget sci-fi films was director Robert Wise's ***The Day the Earth Stood Still*** (1951), which imposed both a liberal and a biblical agenda on this nervous planet, while leavening the doomsday message with the healing touch of a mother and son.

From a spaceship that lands in Washington, DC's President's Park comes Klaatu (Michael Rennie), a human-looking emissary from a more advanced species than ours, and his oversize robot Gort. He says he has come in peace, but a nervous U.S. soldier shoots him. Escaping from a military hospital, Klaatu assumes the pseudonym "Mr. Carpenter" and takes lodging at a boardinghouse, where he befriends war widow Helen Benson (Patricia Neal) and her son, Bobby (Billy Gray). Bobby takes his stately guest to the Lincoln Memorial and to the home of a world-renowned scientist the boy happens to know. During a global shutdown of electrical power—the half hour the Earth stands still—Klaatu confides his identity to Helen and says that, should he be apprehended, she must sneak onto the spaceship and give Gort this message: "Klaatu *barada nikto*." To save the world, he trusts not in government officials but in a mother with a kind face and an open mind.

Behind Bernard Herrmann's eerie theremin music and the pulp poetry of a robot carrying a pretty woman into a spaceship, *The Day the Earth Stood Still* is a parable of Christ returning to Earth with an apocalyptic warning. Adapting Harry Bates's 1940 story "Farewell to the Master," screenwriter Edmund H. North turned Klaatu into the alien Messiah. His Earth name is Carpenter (Jesus's trade); he dies and rises again; and like so many movie Christs, he has an elegant bone structure and a posh English accent. He also befriends a woman whom others would ignore: Helen is a sinless Mary Magdalene. When her boyfriend Tom (Hugh Marlowe) gets jealous and informs the government, Helen breaks off their relationship. She presumably kept Tom around to be a father figure to Bobby. Now the boy has the ultimate role model: God the Son. But Klaatu's final message carries some of the Old Testament God's severity. All nations must live in peace, he proclaims. But if our military belligerence extends into outer space, then robots like Gort will destroy the Earth. "The decision rests with you." In other words, try to be as peaceful as we, your superiors, are—or we'll kill you.

Sci-fi mothers often found themselves drawn to celestial powers. In Steven Spielberg's ***Close Encounters of the Third Kind*** (1977), the mission of single mom Jillian Guiler (Melinda Dillon) is simply to find her missing four-year-old Barry (Cary Guffey). First he wanders to a hillside where strangers have convened to hear a plangent astral melody; then he is abducted—in fact, briefly adopted—by aliens, propelling Jillian and fellow searcher Roy Neary (Richard Dreyfuss) on a trip that culminates in the first official meeting of humankind and extraterrestrials. Barry has hitched a ride on a starship, to be returned unharmed to his mother. This vision of alien benignity pays heartfelt homage to the spirit of early Disney features, not only in its use of the *Pinocchio* song "When You Wish Upon a Star" but also in its childlike belief in the magic of movies and in the precious link between mother and son. Spielberg built on this domestic innocence in 1982's ***E.T. the Extra-Terrestrial***, where Dee Wallace as the divorced mother is the top-billed performer. The story, though, is really about her boy Elliott (Henry

E.T. the Extra-Terrestrial, 1982: Suburban mom Dee Wallace and daughter
Drew Barrymore are witnesses to the closest encounter of all.

Thomas) and his very special pal—another godlike being who befriends an anxious mother's sensitive son.

The New Woman meets the Man of Iron in ***The Terminator***. A humanoid robot (who but Arnold Schwarzenegger?) has taken a trip back from the mid-twenty-first century to the movie's present time (when but 1984?) to try to reverse the history of the future. A man named John Connor is destined to lead the survivors of a nuclear war to victory over evil machines like Arnold—*if* a woman named Sarah Connor (Linda Hamilton) lives long enough to give birth. While the automaton Arnold goes on his mission to perform a "retroactive abortion," another time traveler, Kyle Reese (Michael Biehn), follows him to save John's prospective mother and terminate the Terminator. Aside from its kick-ass thriller energy, James Cameron's movie is a hip

retelling of the Annunciation: Sarah is a secular Virgin Mary, John is her divine son and Reese is the messenger angel sent to impregnate Sarah with the holy word. Hamilton imbues Sarah with an indomitable maternal protectiveness of the child she may not as yet have conceived. The New Testament vibe continues in Cameron's 1991 sequel

The Terminator, 1984: Waitress Sarah Connor (Linda Hamilton) asks, "Do I look like the mother of the future?"

Terminator 2: Judgment Day, which sends Sarah and the teenage John (Edward Furlong) on the sci-fi equivalent of the Holy Family's flight into Egypt.

However odd it seems to propose the five-times-married Cameron as a feminist filmmaker, he has filled almost all his stories (*The Abyss*, *True Lies*, *Titanic*, *Avatar*) with strong, or at least headstrong, women. In **Aliens**, the 1986 sequel to Ridley Scott's 1979 sci-fi horror thriller, Cameron set up the ultimate fantasy confrontation between two righteous single mothers: the earthling heroine Ripley (Sigourney Weaver) and a mammoth bug—the matriarch of the creatures killing off the *Sulaco*'s crew members. In the first film, Ripley had shown protective affection only for her cat, Jones. Now she has taken maternal responsibility for Newt (Carrie Henn), an orphan who tells Ripley, "My mommy always said there were no monsters, no real ones. But there are." The main monster is the alien queen, on a mission to protect her slavering, devouring and, as she sees it, endangered young. When the queen goes for Newt, Ripley slips inside the exoskeleton of a forklift power loader to wage war, one mother against another. When she saves and hugs Newt, the girl calls her "Mommy."

Ripley, a character that Weaver puckishly nicknamed "Rambolina," applies mother wit as well as a warrior's will to defeating her giant-insect rival. That combination makes her the definitive heroine in science-fiction action pictures. In an age that rewards strength over grace, let there be women as strong as Ripley. May homeless children have no less determined an adoptive mother; may extraterrestrial predators meet no less wily an antagonist. Trust moviegoers to detect the glamorous resolve beneath the smudges and sweat on Ripley's face and the feral humor in her challenge to Big Mama Alien: "Get away from her, you bitch!"

In director Zack Snyder's **Man of Steel** (2013), the twelve-year-old Clark Kent (Dylan Sprayberry) saves a school bus from disaster and, more horrifying, discovers he has X-ray vision that gives him an inside look at death; it's like the

facing page: Aliens, 1986: A devoted surrogate mom (Sigourney Weaver) defends little Newt (Carrie Henn) against one big bad mother.

most violent onset of puberty. Understandably traumatized, he locks himself in a Smallville school closet. His mother Martha (Diane Lane) arrives, but the boy is still empowered by panic: he turns the outside doorknob glowing hot, until Martha's calming words about his special nature reduce his fears. For Clark, this episode provides a revelatory lightning flash of his Otherness.

But the parents who found him as an infant in a spaceship have known from the start that he's different: he is Kal-El, a superior, indeed supreme being, sent from another planet by his loving parents Jor-El (Russell Crowe) and Lara (Ayelet Zurer). Martha and her husband, Jonathan (Kevin Costner), have decided that the best way to raise this superman is as a normal American kid. Under their gentle tutelage, Clark (played as an adult by Henry Cavill) will learn to reconcile the Krypton divinity of his nature with the Kansas humanity of his nurture.

This movie takes its cue from Bryan Singer's 2006 film *Superman Returns*, which posited our hero as the Christian God come to Earth to save humankind: Jesus Christ Superman. As *Man of Steel* screenwriter David S. Goyer noted, "We didn't come up with these allusions of Superman being Christ-like. That's something that's been embedded in the character from the beginning" (since his 1938 debut in *Action Comics*). Goyer goes further, giving the character a backstory reminiscent of the Gospels: the all-seeing father from afar (plus a mother); the Earth parents; the ascetic wandering in his early maturity (forty days in the desert for Jesus, a dozen years in odd jobs for Kal-El); his public life, in which he performs a series of miracles; and then, at age thirty-three, the ultimate test of his divinely human nature. "The fate of your planet rests in your hands," the Holy Ghostly Jor-El, in one of his frequent postmortem visits, tells his only begotten son. You could call *Man of Steel* the psychoanalytical case study of a god-man with a two-father complex.

But whereas the Gospels spent little space on Jesus's early years, *Man of Steel*, being an origins story, devotes its first hour or so to demonstrating that Kal-El/Clark is the sum of the love of his two sets of parents. His birth father and mother sacrificed themselves to give him life away from their dying planet; his Earth mother and father fill him with sensible wisdom. When the nine-year-old Clark worries that "the world's too big," Martha expertly comforts him: "Then make it small. Focus

Man of Steel, 2013: Even Superman (Henry Cavill) needs an earth mother (Diane Lane).

on my voice. Pretend it's an island out in the ocean. Can you see it?" And the boy, soothed and enlightened, says, "I see it." Lane, an uplifting presence in movies since her debut at fourteen in 1979's *A Little Romance*, plays Martha as grave, generous and ferociously protective of her boy, this otherworldly treasure and responsibility. At the climax, after Clark has singlehandedly repelled an attack on Metropolis, Martha displays a mother's abiding concern for her son when she asks, "What are you going to do when you're not saving the world?" (Answer: Go to work at the *Daily Planet*.) He may be Superman, but he will always be her baby.

Mother Wore Tights

in TECHNICOLOR

Starring

BETTY GRABLE

with DAN DAILEY and

MONA FREEMAN · CONNIE MARSHALL

VANESSA BROWN · ROBERT ARTHUR · SARA ALLGOOD
WILLIAM FRAWLEY · RUTH NELSON · ANABEL SHAW

Directed by
WALTER LANG · LAMAR TROTTI
Produced by

Dances staged by
SEYMOUR FELIX & KENNY WILLIAMS
Screen play
by Lamar Trotti

20th
CENTURY-FOX

Costumes designed by
ORRY-KELLY
Based on the book
by Miriam Young

Mother Wore Tights, 1947: Bette Grable and Dan Dailey as the showbiz parents of Mona Freeman

SHOWBIZ MOMS

Tensions at home for ladies in the limelight.

I t's said that everyone has two jobs: her own and show business. Such is the proprietary spell that popular entertainment casts on the mass audience. But when a woman's main job is performing under the spotlight, managing her family can be a burden for all concerned. Movies about showbiz moms detail the grind and the glory, while touching ever so lightly on the social significance of these pioneer working women.

In the 1920s, for example, only one in four women was employed outside the home—usually either in subordinate (secretarial) roles or in positions (nurse, teacher, maid, waitress) that extended the traditional role of motherhood into the workplace. If any job allowed women a chance at equality, even supremacy, it was acting. Ladies of the stage and then the screen became among the world's most famous, loved and desired figures.

Being adored, and sustaining that popularity, was a full-time job. A movie actress might have a six a.m. makeup call; she'd be on the set when she could be driving her daughter to school, and exhausted by early evening, when the parent-teacher conference was scheduled. The life of a stage performer often required living out of suitcases; home was a series of hotels or boardinghouses; showtime for her was bedtime for her kids. It's appropriate that the name of the definitive musical about a showbiz mother and daughter was *Gypsy*—not just because Gypsy Rose Lee was the stripper nom de plume taken by Mama Rose's daughter Louise, but also because women in vaudeville and stock companies were forever on the move. Like it or not, they had the gypsy in their souls.

So *Mother Wore Tights* in a vaudeville act with her husband, and when she went back on the road with him after twice giving birth, she left her daughters in the care of their grandmother. Desertion? No: gamely, and gamly, supporting her family the only way she knows—for Myrtle McKinley Burt is played by all-American pinup girl Betty Grable (with chipper Dan Dailey as her husband, Frank) in the 1947 Fox musical, set in the early twentieth century and based on Miriam Young's rosy reminiscence of her song-and-dance family. The only agitation arises when the elder daughter, Iris (Mona Freeman), falls in love with a well-bred collegiate and is briefly embarrassed that her parents will be performing nearby. Chagrin is fleeting: the young man loves Myrtle as much as her audiences do, and Iris ultimately follows Mother's example by getting married *and* going onstage.

A teenage girl could accept a mother in vaudeville. What of a mother in burlesque? In Rouben Mamoulian's *Applause* (1929), one of the first talking pictures to plunder the full cinematic resources of silent films, heavyset chorines shake their stuff onstage for the lowlifes in the seats. The headliner, Kitty Darling (Helen Morgan), is a true trouper: she gave birth to her daughter April one night directly after a performance. Then she sent the child to a convent school, far from the seedy luminescence

Applause, 1929: Burlesque matron Helen Morgan (far right) titillates the crowd but shocks her prim daughter.

of Manhattan fleshpots. When April (Joan Peers) is seventeen, she visits New York and is ushered into Kitty's theater, where she sees what her mother does for a living, and mortification streaks her face like a tragic mask. Can it get worse? It can and does. The man Kitty has married to give April a father figure assaults the girl with kisses and groping, and insists that she join her mother's tawdry act. April refuses, until the night Kitty dies from taking poison, and April goes on in her place—briefly, before running off with a decent guy who will rescue her from the grimy business of show.

Morgan, the torch singer who starred as Julie in the original 1927 Broadway production of *Show Boat* (and would reprise her role in James Whale's 1936 film version), was only twenty-eight, nine years older than Peers, when she made *Applause*. Yet the star's alcohol abuse added a couple of decades to her appearance. She is no pert twenties flapper; she's all flapped out. When Kitty struts onstage, in a spangled costume open at the front to reveal a tiny brassiere, she almost solicits the insults— "They oughta auction off that faded old blonde!"—shouted by the customers. She endures these leers and Bronx cheers to give the daughter she cherishes a better life than hers. *If only you could realize that I'm abasing myself for* you, *dear*: that was the message of so many showbiz-mother films, from *Applause* to **Blonde Venus** . . .

. . . where Mother wears a gorilla costume. Marlene Dietrich was an icon of Teutonic glamour, whether she performed in tuxedos, tights or, as in this 1932 drama, ape couture, to the tune of "Hot Voodoo," backed by a dozen African-American chorines. As with Kitty in *Applause*, Helen Faraday is working onstage less for the glory than for her family: she must support her chemist husband Ned (Herbert Marshall), who has suffered radium poisoning, and their young son, Johnny (six-year-old Dickie Moore). To raise more money for Ned's treatments she rents herself out to millionaire Nick Townsend (the young Cary Grant), and when the cured Ned returns to discover her infidelity, she flees with her son. The boy loves his mother, though their fugitive life propels them into a Depression-era social spiral, from swank dives to farmhouse to flophouse. They are apprehended, and the boy is taken by his father, who tells Helen, "Stay away from Johnny, for good. Give him a chance to forget you. That's the only way you can be a good mother to him now."

Blonde Venus, 1932: Marlene Dietrich dallies with Cary Grant to support her son, Dickie Moore.

Dietrich's seven films for director Josef von Sternberg established her cool allure as a smiling goddess who made her body available to many men, her heart to few. *Blonde Venus* domesticated Dietrich, making her a loving wife and mother—a woman who betrayed her husband to save his life, and who kidnapped her son to nurture him; between her nightclub shows, she teaches him the alphabet. Oddly, erotic passion informs neither Helen's marriage to Ned nor her affair with Nick. (We repeat:

the young Cary Grant!) Her most intense and playful emotional relationship is with Johnny, whom she cuddles in a hayloft, bathes and kisses . . . bathes *with* kisses. In a life on the run with his mother, the lad finds adventure: "I hope they never find us." And when Helen finally comes home to Ned, Johnny stage-manages their reconciliation. "Aw, you're not doing it right at all," he says, playfully pouting. "You're supposed to kiss each other." Like a kindergarten Sternberg, Johnny is directing his parents to their happy ending.

Mothers, the true auteurs of the children to whom they give birth, tend also to be their directors. And if a woman isn't a stage or screen star, perhaps she can guide her child to the fame that life denied her. "You are my daughter and you can become an actress," says mama Maddalena in Luchino Visconti's **Bellissima** (1952), adding, "I could have done it myself if I'd wanted to." No matter that the open casting call at the Cinecittà studio is for a girl eight to ten, and that tiny Maria (Tina Apicella) is barely six—for Maddalena is played by Anna Magnani, the great Earth Mother of Italian cinema in Roberto Rossellini's *Open City* and *The Miracle*, and Pier Paolo Pasolini's *Mamma Roma*. Who can stop this cyclonic force of nature from securing the ingénue role for her daughter? Not her exasperated working-class husband, nor anyone connected with the film project—nor even Maria, a shy sweetie with no perceptible ambition to see her name in lights. For Maddalena, stardom seems as close as the outdoor movie theater next to her Rome tenement. Some night, she hopes, little Maria will be a giant light on that screen.

At Cinecittà, Maddalena meets Iris, a lovely young woman who appeared in a few films but now can get movie work only as an assistant editor. (Liliana Mancini, the actress playing this role, endured the same career trajectory in her own life.) "Give up your dreams," Iris advises all aspiring performers, "and stick to a real job." A flicker of resignation briefly creases Maddalena's face when she sneaks into a projection booth and overhears the crew making jokes about her daughter's screen test—before she assaults the director with an impassioned aria about the great little actress he is ignoring. In Cesare Zavattini's original script, Maria was denied the role. But such is Magnani's magnificence, as one of the all-time indomitable movie moms, that Visconti decided the only plausible ending was a happy one. *Bellissima* finally

Bellissima, 1952: Soundstage mom Anna Magnani wants her young daughter
(Tina Apicella) to be a star, but it's mother who has the star quality.

reconciles stardom in movies with a mother's belated understanding of her child's needs. Maria gets the part, and Maddalena turns it down. It's enough that the girl is a star in her mother's eyes.

"History," Winston Churchill said, "is written by the victors." But the history of showbiz mothers is written by the survivors: their daughters. Occasionally, those recollections are as sunny as in *Mother Wore Tights*. More often, they brandish an exasperation tinged with affection (*Postcards from the Edge*) and respect (*Gypsy*). And sometimes they serve as acts of revenge for a miserable childhood. Thank you, *Mommie Dearest*.

Joan Crawford won an Oscar for *Mildred Pierce* as the selfless mother of a rancid child. But at the B-movie end of a legendary career, she devolved from screen queen to scream queen by headlining a series of tawdry psychological thrillers. In the first of these, *What Ever Happened to Baby Jane?* (1962), she got to swap torments with another Warner Bros. leading lady, Bette Davis. In two others, *Strait-Jacket* (1964) and *Berserk!* (1967), the Crawford character is suspected of violent murders that turn out to have been committed by her deranged daughter. The reason, in *Berserk!*: years ago, Mother had ignored her little girl, so the grown daughter (Judy Geeson) is getting close to Mom by killing off the competition.

Christina Crawford, whom Joan adopted in 1940 after her divorce from Franchot Tone, certainly wished she had received less attention from Mommie dearest. In the 1981 movie of Christina's memoir, Joan (Faye Dunaway) is both the apotheosis and the parody of the wicked mother figure. She treats the girl (played by Mara Hobel as a child and Diana Scarwid as an adult) like a scullery maid; she demeans her, beats her, nearly chokes her to death. No less hurtful is Joan's trick of seeming the victim—"You *love* to make me hit you!"—to a daughter whose fear and devotion she demands in equal doses. When she insisted that Christina call her "mommie dearest," Faye's Joan says, "I wanted you to mean it."

Whether the charges are Bible-true or exaggerated from spite (Christina, who also became an actress, published the book a year after she learned she had been cut

Mommie Dearest, 1981: Faye Dunaway as Joan Crawford and Mara Hobel as the actress's adopted daughter, Christina.

out of Joan's will), director Frank Perry's movie lurches between inside-Hollywood exposé and a catalog of child abuse, between operatic high camp and a Joan Crawford horror movie. (Joan, in the rose garden: "Tina, bring me the axe!") In the infamous scene of Joan whupping the young Christina with a wire coat hanger, Dunaway is photographed from below and in moody lighting as a classic monster from the closet. Unlike many over-the-top performances, this one is not a pleasure but an ordeal to watch—a scary-great turn, up there with Anthony Perkins's in the monster-mother film *Psycho*. So indelible was the connection of these stars to these roles that they were instantly defined by them, and their careers never quite recovered.

Gypsy, from its Broadway premiere in 1959, had a more benign effect on starring actresses: it extended their éclat through middle age and beyond. Ethel Merman created the role of Mama Rose, who shepherds her two daughters through vaudeville until Louise emerges as Gypsy Rose Lee and June as actress June Havoc. Angela Lansbury, Tyne Daly, Bernadette Peters and Patti LuPone headlined Broadway revivals of the classic show by author Arthur Laurents, composer Jule Styne and lyricist Stephen Sondheim.

This is the primal tale of showbiz striving—bad breaks, no breaks, heartbreak, then the big break—that is also a kind of backstage *Gone With the Wind*: the period drama of a woman whose hurricane will triumphs over all obstacles and all those she wants to love her. Like a shark, Rose has a single mission: to push her daughters toward the stardom that fate or circumstance denied her. "I was born too soon," she says, "and started too late." And like Charles Foster Kane, she conflates her function as promoter with her protégé's role onstage. "We're going to be a great opera star," Kane boasted of Susan Alexander. Susan's career flopped, while Gypsy's flourished, allowing Rose to proclaim, "I always promised my daughter we'd be a star."

The starchy 1962 movie replaced Merman with actual Hollywood star Rosalind Russell, who played Rose as an equally bombastic, slightly more acidic cousin of Russell's Auntie Mame (with Natalie Wood as Louise). It remained for Bette Midler, in the 1993 CBS TV film, to put the definitive balls and verve into the part. In the climactic aria "Rose's Turn," Midler summons the ferocity of an oak-strong mother whose daughters have learned from her and left her. "Give 'em love and what does it

Gypsy, 1962: Rosalind Russell as Mama Rose and Natalie Wood as Gypsy Rose Lee.

get you? . . . One quick look as each of 'em leaves you!" Caroming toward madness, Midler's Rose rises to majesty as she gives each line a caress or a curse. She underscores the moral of this "musical fable": that in a family of two girls who became famous performers, Mama really deserved top billing.

"I was such an awful mother," Doris Mann (Shirley MacLaine) says sarcastically to her daughter Suzanne Vale (Meryl Streep), adding, "What if you had a mother like Joan Crawford or Lana Turner?" "These are the options?" Suzanne replies. "You, Joan or Lana?" In Hollywood, kind of. Because ***Postcards from the Edge*** (1990) was based on a novel by Carrie Fisher, the writer and actress whose parents were Debbie Reynolds and Eddie Fisher, audiences were welcome to infer it was the inside dish on her movie-star mom. In fact, this is the tale of two people, who happen to be mother and daughter, learning to accept their vast differences in personality. Think of *Gypsy* siring *Terms of Endearment*.

The novel, written in epistolary form, concentrated more on the dark laughter of the rehab clinic. The movie, scripted by Fisher and directed by Mike Nichols, drops the postcards but keeps the edge in its sympathetic, evenhanded portrayal of two women who must fight their addictions: the daughter to hard drugs, the mother to alcohol (though Doris claims, "Now I just drink like an Irish person") and both to each other. Neither is the villain or the heroine. Suzanne might love to blame all her woes on her mother, but a wise director (Gene Hackman) gives her some advice that is applicable to all children. "I don't know your mother," he says, "but I'll tell you something. She did it to you and her mother did it to her and back and back and back all the way to Eve, and at some point you just say, 'F— it, I start with me.'"

Postcards starts and ends with the family ties of women who get on each other's nerves, like some feuding vaudeville duo, and, despite or because of that abrasion, are great company. Streep, in one of her few daughter roles, catches Suzanne's exhaustion and impatience with a mother who's too much of a kooky character to hate. MacLaine, in a role that Reynolds wanted to play, softens her *Terms of Endearment* mom

facing page: Gypsy, 1993: Everything's coming up Bette Midler!

Postcards from the Edge, 1990: Shirley MacLaine and Meryl Streep as a most theatrical mother and daughter.

with a plethora of frailties. She also brandishes her musical chops with a wonderfully fulsome rendition of Sondheim's *Follies* song "I'm Still Here": "First you're another sloe-eyed vamp, / Then someone's mother, then you're camp." In *Postcards* she is all of these. Better still, she finds an aging woman's tenacious grimace under decades of gamine makeup.

Doris and Suzanne, and MacLaine and Streep, duel to a draw in the titanic battle of mother and daughter—not just in show business clans but often in the lives of people we know—to determine which one is the family's true, incandescent presence. And at the end they realize that a family, like a movie, can have two great stars.

The Greatest Mama of Them All

Mama Rose inspires all of us whose hearts lie in performing. You don't quit. You don't whine. You just go on, and pretty soon, "Everything's Coming Up Roses."

Gypsy is my favorite musical. Every song by Jule Styne and Stephen Sondheim is memorable. It has also given us numerous great tour de force performances. There have been many versions of this musical mother-daughter story, starring the likes of Bernadette Peters, Tyne Daly, Bette Midler. Each has brought varied nuances to the showbiz tyrant who will stop at nothing to achieve stardom for her children. I was always enthralled with Rosalind Russell's brittle film performance. Sure, Ethel Merman owned the Broadway production. She was the original—the barking mama who drove her children to succeed at all costs. We have all come to love and hate her. After all, she was a monster, right? Or was she?

I saw the 1962 film *Gypsy* (directed by Mervyn LeRoy) many times on television. It seemed to play in heavy rotation with *Auntie Mame* (1958). I often got the films confused because they both starred Rosalind Russell playing a dysfunctional, kooky showbiz mom or surrogate mom. I loved the theatrical mother she played in *Mame* and I loved the vulnerability and sacrifice she brought to *Gypsy*. Rosalind Russell's Mama Rose is the driving force, the beating heart, the blood and sweat of showbizness. She instilled in her children, Baby June and Gypsy Rose Lee, that someday their ship would come in, but before it did they had eight shows a week and two on Sunday, so they had to "sing out, Louise! Sing out!"

Mama Rose—both the historical woman and the many fictional portrayals—was the ultimate stage mother because she sacrificed the love of her children for the love of the audience. I like to think that a child's responsibility is to come through for his or her parents, to see their frailties and supplement their dreams. Mama Rose loved her children, but she simply loved show business more. Couldn't they forgive her for that? Sure, she did make them do that lousy act with the cow, but to me those two kids just seemed ungrateful. After all, she got them out of burlesque! They were playing the Orpheum circuit! What were they carping about in "If Mama Was Married"? If Mama was married, they would never have learned the time step or that "You Gotta Have a Gimmick" with those interesting stripper ladies! In short, they wouldn't have made it without their mother's drive and ambition.

Maybe that's what they resented. The symbiotic relationship that drew them together and pulled them apart. Fame.

The culminating moment in *Gypsy* is the confrontation between Mama Rose and her elder daughter, now a star, Gypsy Rose Lee. In the film, daughter Natalie Wood, clad in white fur, accuses her mother of driving her and sister Baby June to be successful because she—Mama Rose—never could be. It's the first time you actually see Mama Rose cry. Her years of toil as a stage mother have left her haggard, unsure of who she really is. In the end, she is neither rewarded nor loved for her sacrifice. Both of her children have rejected her. Left alone onstage, she contemplates if it was worth it. And then what does Mama Rose do? She dries her tears and sings the show-stopper of all time. Curtain up. Light the lights. It's "Rose's Turn."

—*Illeana Douglas*

Terms of Endearment, 1983: Shirley MacLaine and Debra Winger swim in the turbulent flow of mother-daughter love.

A GALLERY OF
MODERN MOMS

*In the last forty years, these very contemporary
stars kept the torch of motherhood burning.*

Forty is a dangerous stage in a film actress's career; fifty could be a death knell. Once Hollywood stardom was gynocentric, but for the last few decades it has been guy-ocentric, allowing male stars to go on exuding their macho musk forever. For actresses, "mid" often means "the end"; they are discarded, while the latest vixen is promoted. If they find a reprieve, it is usually playing mother roles. That's how Shirley MacLaine has extended her movie career to nearly a half century, how Ellen Burstyn keeps honorably and Emmy-winningly employed forty years after *The Exorcist*. Sally Field and Meryl Streep have been playing mothers, and earning Oscars for them, since the late seventies—around the same time that Susan Sarandon reaped shock and admiration for her work as a prostitute mom in *Pretty Baby*. Let the Stallones and Schwarzeneggers go on impersonating surly studs into their Medicare years. These great ladies will take roles that connect with real people on the screen and in the audience.

SHIRLEY MACLAINE

A Broadway dancer in her teens and a movie star at twenty-one in Alfred Hitchcock's *The Trouble with Harry*, MacLaine spread the charm of a soiled but resolute gamine through a decade of memorable films—*Some Came Running*, *The Apartment*, *Irma La Douce* (with an Oscar nomination for each of these three). Radiating too much independence to be a submissive-daughter type in Hollywood films, she proved in her forties to be a dynamite movie mom. Her facility with both light comedy and dark drama prepared her for the emotional teeterboard of Deedee in **The Turning Point** (1977), a woman whose daughter's rise in the ballet world tests her decision, when she was young, to give up her career for marriage. MacLaine's delicate equipoise between a mother's pride and a dancer's regret resulted in her fourth Best Actress nomination.

Fifth time was the charm, with a win as Aurora Greenway in **Terms of Endearment** (1983), James L. Brooks's adaptation of the Larry McMurtry novel about a woman who nearly crushes her daughter Emma (Debra Winger) with maternal love. Spanning three decades, this warmly episodic film saunters through Aurora's widowhood, Emma's marriage and the turbulent flow of mother-daughter bonding and bondage. Epic emotions play out on an intimate scale as the two women get in each other's way and heart. Opposing forces of nature, they naturally dominate their men: Jack Nicholson as Aurora's astronaut beau ("I was just inches from a clean getaway") and Jeff Daniels as Emma's unworthy husband ("I mean, who am I if I'm not the man who's failing Emma?").

As in 1990's *Postcards from the Edge* (see the chapter "Showbiz Moms"),

MacLaine got the showier role and was showered in acclaim, all deserved. *Terms of Endearment* delivers an emotional body blow toward the end, when the actress nimbly pirouettes from outsize comedy to subtle pathos and reveals the pain behind Aurora's grand gestures. MacLaine would find use for them thirty years later, as the brassy American mother of Countess Crawley (Elizabeth McGovern) in the British serial drama *Downton Abbey* and, deglamorized, as Ben Stiller's earthy mom in *The Secret Life of Walter Mitty*. You needn't be a believer in reincarnation to suspect that MacLaine will go on dancing forever.

SALLY FIELD

Even as TV's Gidget and the Flying Nun in her teens and early twenties, she was great mother material. The apple cheeks framing an incandescent smile suggested a generosity that Field, in her mature roles, could pass on to her movie children. From her Emmy-winning role in *Sybil* (1976), where she played a woman who created more than a dozen personalities to erase an abused childhood, she graduated to film stardom, and her first Best Actress Oscar, as a North Carolina textile worker in ***Norma Rae*** (1979). A widowed mother of two who cares for her own mother, going deaf from the noise in the mill, Norma Rae realizes, thanks to a New York labor organizer (Ron Liebman), that she harbors the spirit of a heroic maternal figure: Mary Harris "Mother" Jones, who helped win livable working conditions for Pennsylvania miners. The adorably feisty Field shows how a woman who never thought herself more than ordinary, and whose prime weekend recreation is soaking her tired feet, can give birth to a passion for social justice.

Field earned her second Oscar for ***Places in the Heart*** (1984), writer-director Robert Benton's poignant memory film of his own mother in Depression-era Waxahachie, Texas. Widowed when a wandering drunk kills her sheriff husband, Edna Spalding must raise her two young children and bring the family cotton crop to market, helped only by a blind man (John Malkovich) and a black man (Danny Glover). Lending a bit of her autobiography to Edna, Field engenders an aura of communal resolve that prepares the viewer for the final scene: an amazing grace

Places in the Heart, 1984: Widowed mother Sally Field fights to save her farm and raise her two kids (Gennie James and Yankton Hatten).

of reconciliation. As calmly resolute as she was in *Places in the Heart*, Field adroitly switched to empathetic agitation in *Steel Magnolias* (1989) as a woman who must watch and worry as her diabetic daughter (Julia Roberts) risks her life to bear a child. She played another woman with an unusual child as the loving, supportive mother in **Forrest Gump** (1994). If the IQ-challenged Forrest (Tom Hanks) had the good luck to stumble into every headline event in forty years of American history, it is because his mother honed and home-cooked that Alabama boy's preternaturally sweet soul.

The core of her Mary Todd Lincoln in Steven Spielberg's **Lincoln** (2012) was less nurturing than nudging: advising her president husband (Daniel Day-Lewis) on political tactics and pleading with him to keep their son Robert (Joseph Gordon-Levitt) from joining the Union Army. "She was complicated and brilliant," Field has said of Mrs. Lincoln, "and she would not be looked at fondly." The actress has given brilliant, often complicated performances over her half-century career. Really, though, what viewer doesn't look at Sally Field fondly?

ELLEN BURSTYN

After purging the devil from your young daughter, in **The Exorcist** (see the chapter "Crime and Horror Moms"), what's a mother to do? Leave your New Mexico home and drive your eleven-year-old kid with the R-rated mouth toward California to pursue your unlikely dream as a singer—and get stuck slinging hash at Mel's Diner. In Martin Scorsese's mother-son road movie **Alice Doesn't Live Here Anymore** (1974), Burstyn's Alice tried balancing threats with affection, often in a single tirade. When Tommy (Alfred Lutter III) wonders for the zillionth time, "Are we in Arizona yet?" Alice explodes into "If you ask me that one more time, I'm gonna beat you to death," then, as if instantly exorcised, adds, "Just sit back there and relax and enjoy life, huh?" Monitoring this exchange, any parent (or child) could say, "Yep, that's me." Robert Getchell's screenplay, while nailing the bonhomie of waitresses and acknowledging the violent eruptions of which quiet men are capable, dawdles in a few clichés, like the dreamboat (Kris Kristofferson) waiting for Alice in the final reels. Yes, he loves Alice, and he even likes her kid.

Alice Doesn't Live Here Anymore, 1974: Ellen Burstyn gets a cold one from her son, Alfred Lutter III.

An adventurous actress, Burstyn appeared in a naughty movie version of Henry Miller's *Tropic of Cancer* the year before breaking out in **The Last Picture Show** (1971), the Peter Bogdanovich film of another Larry McMurtry novel. She is Lois Farrow, once the reigning beauty of Anarene, Texas, who married a poor boy and "scared [him] into getting rich." Her daughter, Jacy (Cybill Shepherd), who has assumed the crown, figures she can prod the same success out of her beau Duane (Jeff Bridges), but Mom is skeptical: "You're not scary enough." They share something, though: the bed of a local oilman (Clu Gulager). Like mother, like daughter, perhaps even on the same night.

Lois was a nun compared to Sara Goldfarb in Darren Aronofsky's **Requiem for a Dream** (2000). The first line of Hubert Selby Jr.'s source novel—"Harry locked his mother in the closet"—gets to the essence of two warring addicts: Sara, the Blanche DuBois or Mary Tyrone of Brighton Beach, and her son (Jared Leto). They're made for each other: Mom swears by amphetamines and TV hucksters; Harry loves heroin and, to buy it, steals her TV set. By the time the crash-dieting Sara starts hallucinating that her refrigerator is clambering through the kitchen to devour her, Burstyn has woven strands of madness into a brave and mesmerizing distillation of paranoia. She takes the viewer on a jolting trip through the theme park called hell.

SUSAN SARANDON

Utterly, sumptuously at ease under the eye of the camera, Sarandon finds a star's equilibrium between the personality she is and the person she's bringing to the screen. No one else in films manages to be so regal and so egalitarian. From her movie debut in *Joe*, through her early prime in *The Rocky Horror Picture Show, Atlantic City, The Hunger* and *The Witches of Eastwick* and up to the four roles across the millennia she played in the Wachowskis' *Cloud Atlas*, Sarandon has been the American cinema's beacon of erotic intelligence: our own Statue of Libertine. She's got the advantage of those expressive orbs; young moviegoers, asked to conjure up the memory of Bette Davis, might say she had Susan Sarandon eyes. But it's her mouth that sets

The Last Picture Show, 1971: Ellen Burstyn and Cybill Shepherd in a Prom Queen battle of the generations.

the tone; it seems ever on the verge of a smile, as if she understands that our lives may end in tragedy, but we're myopic if we don't see the fun in it.

Gravity mixes with the comedy in Sarandon's attitude. She has the range to be big sister (*Thelma & Louise*), both manager and Madame (*Bull Durham*) and doting, crackpot mom (*Anywhere But Here*). She was Ariel, a very earthy sprite, in Paul Mazursky's Shakespeare update *Tempest*. In the past dozen years, older but no less alluring, she has movie-mothered Jake Gyllenhaal (*Moonlight Mile*), Shia LaBeouf (*Wall Street: Money Never Sleeps*), Orlando Bloom (*Elizabethtown*), Rachel Weisz (*The Lovely Bones*), Liv Tyler (*Robot & Frank*), Jason Segal and Ed Helms (*Jeff, Who Lives at Home*) and her own daughter Eva Amurri (*Middle of Nowhere*). Yet she earned her Oscar playing a nun (in *Dead Man Walking*) whose faith and spirituality glow like God's love light.

She boldly redefined the movies' notion of motherhood in Louis Malle's **Pretty Baby** (1978). Her Hattie was a New Orleans prostitute with a twelve-year-old daughter—Brooke Shields in the flush of her nymphancy—and an ethical obtuseness more shocking than the silk and sizzle of her exposed flesh. (The same year, Sarandon and Shields reunited as American-Romany mother and daughter in *King of the Gypsies*.) In George Miller's **Lorenzo's Oil**, from 1992, a Sarandon character faces one of her gravest challenges. She and Nick Nolte play a married couple suckerpunched by fate: their son has a dreadful disease, whose incurability the wife is loath to accept. The parents share an intimate closeup, nearly three minutes long, whose focus gradually shifts from Nolte describing the disease to Sarandon's dawning dread as she realizes the consequences. Tears drop simultaneously from both eyes, as if the last of this mother's illusions had been squeezed out of her. It is a devastating scene, played with spectacular subtlety.

We should also remember Sarandon for an overlooked performance in an underappreciated film: the Wachowskis' **Speed Racer** (2008). In this technologically precocious fable of the little man fighting the big corporation, Pops Racer (John Goodman) is a mechanic turned car designer and his son Speed (Emile Hirsch) is the youngster ready to win the big rallies against a rigged system. Sarandon plays

Lorenzo's Oil, 1992 : Susan Sarandon helps research a cure for the rare disease afflicting her son (Zack O'Malley Greenburg).

Mom, the family's emotional center and a font of dewy sagacity. Mom seems utterly at home in the Wachowskis' hallucinogenic reimagining of the 1950s *Father Knows Best* as a Tex Avery cartoon. And like a good '50s mother, she is her son's biggest fan and the source of his cheerful determination. Of Speed's mastery behind the wheel, she says it is "inspiring and beautiful, and everything art should be." We could say the same about the forty-plus-year career of Susan Sarandon.

MERYL STREEP

The most honored actress—or actor—of her generation, Dame Meryl has also been Mama Meryl, in a dozen or so movies, almost since the beginning of her film career. In 1979 she costarred with Dustin Hoffman in ***Kramer vs. Kramer*** and

The Manchurian Candidate, 2004: The credenza gives bat wings to Eleanor Shaw (Meryl Streep), manipulative mother of Raymond Shaw (Liev Schreiber).

won her first Oscar in the chilly role of a mother who walks out on her husband and eight-year-old son. Streep's second Oscar came for *Sophie's Choice* (1982), in which William Styron's Polish woman, trapped in the Nazi Holocaust, faces the awful decision of which of her children she must consign to death. Streep's blond, aristocratic affect and the hauteur of her cheekbones have allowed her to play all manner of mothers who are suspect because she looks so darned smart. She was Lindy Chamberlain, the Australian woman unjustly convicted of murdering the baby she said was abducted by a dingo, in *A Cry in the Dark* (1988). In *Marvin's Room* (1996) she was the selfish mother of a troubled child—a definition that, if raised to nuclear proportions, might fit her Eleanor Shaw in the 2004 remake of *The Manchurian Candidate*. No son, no domestic or foreign government, is safe from the toxic touch of Eleanor, who, in Streep's satirical turn, oddly resembled the then junior senator from New York: Hillary Clinton.

Tackling any role in the belief she can wrestle behavioral truth out of it—for example, the lesbian mother of Claire Danes in *The Hours* (2002)—Streep has also submerged herself in many genres. She became an action figure, an expert rafter protecting her young son against two killers in *The River Wild* (1994). She sang country music as Shirley MacLaine's daughter in *Postcards from the Edge*; played Lindsay Lohan's country-singing mom in the Robert Altman movie based on Garrison Keillor's radio show *A Prairie Home Companion* (2006); and, in *Mamma Mia!* (2008), sang ABBA hits while juggling three suitors, arranging her daughter's wedding and nearly exploding with manic energy. Over-the-top is just the launch pad for her turn as the cancer-ridden matriarch in the 2013 film of the Pulitzer-winning play *August: Osage County*. Hers is the loudest performance but not the most acute: Julia Roberts and Julianne Nicholson as her daughters, and Margo Martindale as her sister, all do work more grounded and less histrionic.

A taut, naturalistic Streep is on view in *. . . First Do No Harm* (1997), a fact-based TV movie that she produced as well as starred in. Playing the mother of an epileptic child, Streep searches for treatments her doctor will not prescribe and juggles questions of aching financial need, the humiliations of the newly poor, the sight of kids crying while the parents argue over huge hospital bills. She has the small

Mamma Mia!, 2008: Meryl Streep, with Amanda Seyfried, sings her way into her daughter's heart.

gestures and tight, hectoring voice of a woman untrained for conflict, and, finally, the exhaustion of a longtime caregiver. Here she shows that great acting can be the sum of the most minute calibrations, in a character who overcomes emotional exhaustion to attain domestic heroism.

Tyler Perry's Madea: an old-fashioned matriarch for the twenty-first century.